Green Budget Tagging

INTRODUCTORY GUIDANCE & PRINCIPLES

OECD
BETTER POLICIES FOR BETTER LIVES

This work is published under the responsibility of the Secretary-General of the OECD. The opinions expressed and arguments employed herein do not necessarily reflect the official views of OECD member countries.

This document, as well as any data and map included herein, are without prejudice to the status of or sovereignty over any territory, to the delimitation of international frontiers and boundaries and to the name of any territory, city or area.

The statistical data for Israel are supplied by and under the responsibility of the relevant Israeli authorities. The use of such data by the OECD is without prejudice to the status of the Golan Heights, East Jerusalem and Israeli settlements in the West Bank under the terms of international law.

Note by Turkey
The information in this document with reference to "Cyprus" relates to the southern part of the Island. There is no single authority representing both Turkish and Greek Cypriot people on the Island. Turkey recognises the Turkish Republic of Northern Cyprus (TRNC). Until a lasting and equitable solution is found within the context of the United Nations, Turkey shall preserve its position concerning the "Cyprus issue".

Note by all the European Union Member States of the OECD and the European Union
The Republic of Cyprus is recognised by all members of the United Nations with the exception of Turkey. The information in this document relates to the area under the effective control of the Government of the Republic of Cyprus.

Please cite this publication as:
OECD (2021), *Green Budget Tagging: Introductory Guidance & Principles*, OECD Publishing, Paris, *https://doi.org/10.1787/fe7bfcc4-en*.

ISBN 978-92-64-58553-9 (print)
ISBN 978-92-64-54778-0 (pdf)

Preface

Governments are striving to address the twin challenges of responding to the COVID-19 pandemic while taking action in response to the threats posed by climate change. Today, we are given a unique opportunity to bring these agendas together by developing robust recovery packages that restore economic growth in the short term and helping to re-orientate economies towards the low-carbon transition in the medium to longer term. However, navigating this pathway requires countries to take bold action. Governments need to show leadership and develop innovative ways of working to ensure that the decisions we take support forward-looking policies and foster greater resilience in the future. In this context, *Green Budget Tagging Guidance and Principles* looks at how to design and implement an approach to green budget tagging; one that helps each country identify budget measures that will help achieve climate and environmental objectives.

Green budgeting and its component tools, such as green budget tagging, offer a new way for governments to ensure that budget decisions help advance our common goal to tackle climate change, and better protect biodiversity and the environment. The OECD continues to be a leader in supporting the development of green budgeting. In December 2017, we launched the Paris Collaborative on Green Budgeting at the One Planet Summit, to introduce innovative tools to assess and drive improvements in the alignment of national expenditure and revenue processes with climate and other environmental goals. The development of this introductory guidance represents a crucial step forward in helping countries equip themselves with tools that can form the central pillars of an effective approach to green budgeting.

Green budget tagging is a particularly helpful tool in raising awareness of how budget decisions are linked to national objectives. It also provides information that can be used to improve the effectiveness of government action in achieving these objectives. By increasing the visibility of government action, green budget tagging can help both mobilise resources and improve the transparency and accountability of government policy by facilitating better monitoring and reporting. This process also helps countries make progress on their international commitments, such as the National Determined Contributions as part of the Paris Agreement.

This guidance has been developed by the OECD, with the participation and collaboration of the broader community of institutions working in the area of green budgeting. These include the World Bank, the United Nations Development Programme, the Inter-American Development Bank and the International Monetary Fund, all of whom are partners under Principle 4 of the Coalition of Finance Ministers for Climate Action. Furthermore, because the guidance was developed in consultation with Coalition countries, it also reflects and illustrates practices grounded in experiences to date. It does not aim to stipulate a single set of practices, but instead sets out the options for embedding a coherent approach – as a first step. The reader is provided a valuable and useful tool, serving as an introductory guide for basic questions and crucial issues in designing and implementing an effective approach to green budget tagging. We very much hope that this Guidance helps governments take the budget decisions necessary to advance toward both their national and international climate and environmental objectives.

Angel Gurría
Secretary-General, OECD

Foreword

The OECD's Green Budgeting Framework (2020) sets out the building blocks underpinning an effective approach to green budgeting, including tools that can be used to help build an evidence base and support policy coherence. There is growing momentum for the use of green budget tagging as one of the core tools of green budgeting. Countries see its potential to help mobilise a more targeted fiscal response to climate and environmental challenges. However, putting green budget tagging into practice can sometimes be rather daunting. How do you design a tagging framework? What elements of the budget should be tagged? How should the information gathered through tagging be reported and used in decision making?

Green budget tagging is still a relatively new practice. The United Nations Development Programme developed useful guidance on climate budget tagging, *Knowing What You Spend*, drawing significantly on early experiences in Asia. However, there is now a growing body of experience across Africa, Latin America, the Caribbean and the OECD in relation to green budget tagging.

This introductory guidance builds on existing work and draws together lessons from this wider range of experiences in response to calls from the Paris Collaborative on Green Budgeting to the Coalition of Finance Ministers for Climate Action. It also expands the existing discussion beyond climate budget tagging to green budget tagging, giving insight into how tagging can help support the achievement of environmental objectives beyond those related to climate. It aims to help countries seeking to establish new green budget tagging practices by addressing a set of initial questions when considering options for the design and implementation of an effective approach.

Acknowledgements

The OECD would like to thank the Coalition of Finance Ministers for Climate Action and the institutional partners working under Helsinki Principle 4 – the Inter-American Development Bank (IADB), the International Monetary Fund (IMF), the World Bank and the United Nations Development Programme (UNDP) – for their collaboration in the preparation of this introductory guidance. Particular thanks goes to Raúl Delgado (IADB), Manal Fouad and Claude Wendling (IMF), Adrian Fozzard and Xenia Kirchhofer (World Bank), and Thomas Beloe and Asad Maken (UNDP) for all of their support and input.

In preparation for this report, the OECD conducted consultations with Colombia, France, Ireland and Italy. In addition, the OECD participated in roundtable discussions, organised by the UNDP, with countries across Asia, Africa, Latin America and the Caribbean, including Chile, Ecuador, Ghana, Indonesia, Kenya, Kyrgyzstan, Nepal, Nigeria, Pakistan, the Philippines, Rwanda and Uganda. The Introductory Guidance also includes feedback from independent experts. The authors would like to express their appreciation to all of these stakeholders for their availability and insights.

This report was prepared by Scherie Nicol and Andrew Park of the Public Management and Budgeting Division in the Directorate for Public Governance. The report has also benefited from valuable input from the OECD's Environment Directorate, with special mention to Mauro Migotto, Mireille Martini, Myriam Linster, Kathleen Dominique, Katia Karousakis and Nicolina Lamhauge for their expertise. The OECD is grateful to all of the parties who provided feedback on the report.

Table of contents

3.2.2. Using information to improve the performance of government policy 38
3.3. Using information to qualify for green finance instruments 39
3.4. Ensuring the results of green budgeting are transparent and open to independent oversight ... 39

4. Key challenges in designing and implementing green budget tagging 42
4.1. Identifying the appropriate level of granularity for tagging 42
4.2. Deciding how to deal with budget measures relating to disaster risk management and adaptation 43
4.3. Tagging negative budget measures 43
4.4. Ensuring consistency and quality of tagging 44
4.5. Balancing environmental, social and economic objectives 45

5. Elements that can support an effective approach to green budget tagging 46
5.1. Strong political and administrative leadership 46
5.2. A scaled approach to implementation 47
5.3. Ensuring coherence with wider public financial mangement reforms 48
5.4. Complementing green budget tagging with a wider set of government reforms to achieve national goals 49

6. Bringing it all together: Ten principles underpinning an effective approach to green budget tagging 51
The ten principles underpinning an effective approach to green budget tagging 51

Annex A. Country snapshots 53
France 53
Ireland 54
Nepal 55
Philippines 56

References 58

Notes 64

Tables

Table 1. Classifications systems for green budget tagging across select countries 20
Table 2. France's green budget tagging "at a glance" 54
Table 3. Ireland's green budget tagging "at a glance" 55
Table 4. Nepal's green budget tagging "at a glance" 56
Table 5. Philippine's green budget tagging "at a glance" 57

Figures

Figure 1. Key decisions in designing an approach to green budget tagging 16
Figure 2. OECD Green Budgeting Framework 27
Figure 3. Role for evidence from green budgeting at different stages of the budget cycle 38

Boxes

Box 1. Green budgeting 12

Follow OECD Publications on:

》》

[twitter] http://twitter.com/OECD_Pubs

[facebook] http://www.facebook.com/OECDPublications

[linkedin] http://www.linkedin.com/groups/OECD-Publications-4645871

[youtube] http://www.youtube.com/oecdilibrary

[OECD Alerts] http://www.oecd.org/oecddirect/

Abbreviations and acronyms

CBA	Central budget authority
CC	Climate change
CEA	Classification of Environmental Activities
CEPA	Classification of Environmental Protection Activities
COFOG	Classification of the Functions of Government
CPEIR	Climate Public Expenditure and Institutional Review
CReMA	Classification of Resource Management Activities
DAC	Development Assistance Committee
DPER	Department of Public Expenditure and Reform
EU	European Union
GBS	Green budget statement
GBA+	Gender Based Analysis +
GHG	Greenhouse gas
IADB	Inter-American Development Bank
ICMA	International Capital Markets Association
IMF	International Monetary Fund
MDB	Multilateral development bank
NACE	*Nomenclature statistique des activités économiques dans la Communauté européenne* (Statistical Classification of Economic Activities in the European Community)
NDC	Nationally Determined Contribution
PINE	Policy Instruments for the Environment (database)
PFM	Public financial management
R&D	Research and development
SDG	Sustainable Development Goal
UNDP	United Nations Development Programme

Executive summary

Climate change, biodiversity loss and wider environmental degradation are major, imminent threats facing our planet and our societies. International initiatives such as the Paris Agreement, the Aichi Biodiversity Targets under the Convention on Biodiversity and the Sustainable Development Goals are helping governments around the world commit to co-ordinated action. In pursuit of these commitments, many governments have set national goals, unique to their local contexts and capabilities, to help protect the environment (e.g. biodiversity) and mitigate climate change. Public expenditure amounts to a significant proportion of economic activity – thus, government tax and spending decisions can have powerful social, environmental and economic implications for a country. Given that the budget document is the government's central policy document and the important role it plays in determining how resources are allocated to deliver national goals, it is appropriate that priorities related to the environment and climate change be considered as part of the budget process.

Green budgeting offers a range of tools and techniques for governments seeking ways to bring green perspectives to bear on the budget process. One of the central green budgeting tools in many countries is green budgeting tagging. This tool involves assessing each individual budget measure and giving it a "tag" according to whether it is helpful or harmful to green objectives. Green objectives may relate to climate or other areas of the environment, such as biodiversity, air and water challenges (quantity and quality). Information gathered from tagging individual measures can be useful to understand how overall budget policy impacts cross-cutting goals relating to climate and the environment. Lessons from country experiences highlight the diversity of approaches, rooted in the national context but aligned to international commitments (e.g. Nationally Determined Contributions).

Before any country starts green budget tagging, it is helpful to have clarity on why it is being introduced – identifying what "problem" it is trying to solve. This helps in assessing whether or not tagging is indeed the right approach. Designing an approach to green budget tagging requires an awareness of key decisions such as defining what is "green" by taking into consideration national objectives and existing international principles and standards, deciding what budget measures to tag across sectors and administrative levels, developing a classification system to categorise information, and identifying information needs to develop a weighting system that takes into account the relevance of different budget measures.

Given that green budget tagging is still relatively new, countries tend to take an adaptive approach to implementation, allowing the scope and processes to evolve as capacity and familiarity develop over time. Most countries start by tagging expenditures that make a positive contribution to green objectives. However, some countries also tag revenues as well as budget lines that negatively impact green objectives. Approaches vary considerably depending on the political rationale for introducing green budget tagging. Over time, greater convergence on these aspects may emerge and will support cross-country comparisons and analysis.

The information produced by green budget tagging can be powerful when it is fed into policy making and budget decisions. As such, it is important for countries to consider how the information from green budget tagging can be used alongside evidence from other green budgeting tools, such as environmental impact assessments and the application of a green perspective to performance setting and spending review, to inform budget decision making and provide greater accountability and oversight. Ensuring that green budget tagging is more than a paper exercise is also important for generating buy-in for its introduction and development.

Emerging lessons have highlighted key challenges in the implementation of green budget tagging. These include identifying the appropriate level of granularity for tagging; deciding what to do with budget measures related to climate adaptation as distinct from climate mitigation; tagging negative budget items; and balancing trade-offs across environmental, social and economic objectives. Budget tagging is by its nature subjective and requires sound judgements across government, even when there may be incentives to "greenwash" or underestimate relevant budget items as part of the process. As such, it is important to ensure that tagging decisions are open to scrutiny, both internally and externally, with opportunities for oversight by the supreme audit institution, parliament and civil society as part of the larger effort.

Green budget tagging should not be a stand-alone tool, but works most effectively as part of a broader approach to green budgeting with a strong strategic framework (such as relevant strategies, policies and plans that include clear goals for government policy) and a supportive enabling environment (such as capacity development, clear guidance for government stakeholders and suitable financial management information systems). The implementation of green budget tagging will be most effective where there is strong political and administrative leadership, and a scaled approach to its introduction.

On a more strategic level, green budget tagging should be coherent with other public financial management reforms. For example, tagging exercises can complement the implementation of reforms such as performance budgeting or developing a medium-term expenditure framework, since they provide information on financial resources allocated to high-level policy priorities. Implementing tagging alongside a wider set of government actions, such as regulatory reform, green public procurement and the integration of green criteria into cost-benefit analysis for infrastructure investment, are also important for maximising progress towards national climate and environmental goals. A whole-of-government approach encompassing legal, regulatory, policy and budget decisions has significantly more potential to be effective than the implementation of a single, stand-alone tool.

Introduction

There is increasing recognition of the physical and transition risks posed by climate change and environmental degradation. For example, evidence shows that changes in the climate system are contributing to a range of biophysical effects that are already impacting society and the economy. Future impacts are expected to be much greater. Given the cost of inaction, many governments have set national goals to help protect the environment (e.g. biodiversity) and mitigate climate change. Taking action also provides the opportunity to unlock investment and job opportunities associated with a more sustainable economic model.

Public expenditure amounts to a significant proportion of economic activity, thus government spending decisions have powerful social, environmental and economic implications for a country. Along with regulations, the choice and design of tax and expenditure also shape business decisions and influence people's choices to work, invest and consume. Public expenditure also plays a key role in mobilising the private finance necessary to tackle climate change and other environmental challenges. Given that the budget is the government's central policy document and the important role that it plays in determining how resources are allocated to deliver on national goals, it is appropriate that priorities relating to the environment and climate change be considered as part of the budget process. This is one of the reasons that we are seeing the emergence of practices such as "green budgeting" (Box 1) as part of broader efforts to ensure that the budget supports the achievement of environmental and climate objectives.

Box 1. Green budgeting

Green budgeting is a practice which uses the tools of budgetary policy making to help achieve "green" objectives, i.e. those relating to the climate and environmental dimensions such as biodiversity, air quality and water (see Section 1 for further information). There is no one-size fits all approach to green budgeting. Any approach should build on a country's existing public financial management framework and thus be attuned to the strengths and limitations of the existing budgeting process. While by itself green budgeting does not change existing policies, it provides decision makers with a clearer understanding of the overall environmental and climate impacts of budgeting choices. It brings evidence together in a systematic and co-ordinated manner to allow more informed decision making on how to optimise revenue raising and resource allocation in order to fulfil national and international commitments.

Source: OECD (2020[1]).

Green budget tagging can be a useful tool within an overall approach to green budgeting. In the context of budget management systems where it can be difficult to track how budget policy impacts cross-cutting goals, green budget tagging allows countries to identify areas of expenditure and revenue that are helpful or harmful to green objectives. Green budget tagging encompasses any budget tagging practice that seeks to identify budget measures relating to climate and other environmental objectives, such as biodiversity, air and water challenges (quantity and quality), among others. While some countries identify individual budget measures that specifically target green objectives, green budget tagging involves a comprehensive survey of all budgetary measures to identify those that impact green objectives (whether in a positive, neutral or negative way). The information gained from tagging builds a useful evidence base that can help governments improve coherence between budget measures, green goals and commitments to sustainable development. It also serves to improve transparency in relation to the government's budget policy, thus helping stakeholders such as parliamentarians and civil society hold the government to account for its decisions. Budget tagging is not new; it has been applied in relation to other cross-cutting priorities, such as poverty reduction, the Sustainable Development Goals (SDGs) and gender. Green budget tagging can, however, sit alongside these other tagging exercises as part of overall efforts to ensure that the budget serves to deliver outcomes in relation to cross-cutting high-level priorities. This report aims to provide guidance for countries looking to develop an effective approach to green budget tagging, recognising that practices are also likely to vary depending on country-specific objectives in relation to the exercise. It draws together the lessons from the international budgeting community through both the Paris Collaborative on Green Budgeting and the Coalition of Finance Ministers for Climate Action. In-depth information on country experiences was drawn from interviews with members of the Paris Collaborative on Green Budgeting, a series of regional roundtables organised by the United Nations Development Programme and the Inter-American Development Bank, a review and analysis of climate expenditure tagging methodologies (World Bank, forthcoming[2]), and an assessment of the connections across financial and environmental classifications systems (IADB, forthcoming[3]).

Section 1 outlines the key decisions that need to be taken in designing an approach to green budget tagging. Section 2 sets out considerations in implementing green budget tagging. Section 3 identifies how to utilise and integrate information from tagging in the wider budget process. Section 4 highlights key challenges and Section 5 presents elements that can support an effective approach. Finally, information provided in this guidance is brought together and synthesised into Principles for Green Budget Tagging at the end of this document.

1. Developing green budget tagging

Before any country starts green budget tagging, it is important to have clarity on why it is being introduced, specifically what "problem" it is trying to solve, and to make an assessment of whether or not green tagging is indeed the best approach. Once these considerations, or first principles, are clear, the country is in a position to think about designing an appropriate approach. There are also important considerations in relation to deciding when to undertake the tagging exercise during the budget cycle. This section presents the different design choices and their respective merits in the context of differing local needs, capacities and policy environments.

1.1. First principles: Why do green budget tagging and is it the best approach?

Increasing political focus on the costs of climate change and environmental degradation has led governments to consider what options they have to ensure that public policy supports the achievement of green objectives. Given that the budget is the central policy document of any government, public administrations are looking at how they might develop a budget that is more aligned with national green priorities (including country Nationally Determined Contributions [NDCs], explained in Box 2), better understand financing gaps for achieving green objectives and find ways to help prioritise investments with green benefits in decision making. There is also pressure for governments to improve accountability and transparency in relation to actions that they are taking to address green priorities. And some governments may also be subject to reporting requirements relating to how external financing is being spent *vis-à-vis* green objectives, e.g. for sovereign green bonds[1] or donor financing.

Box 2. Nationally Determined Contributions

Following the 2015 Paris Agreement, parties made commitments to mitigate and adapt to the adverse impacts of climate change. Nationally Determined Contributions (NDCs) reflect the commitments made by each party to reduce national emissions and adapt to the impacts of climate change. As such, the NDCs provide long-term goal for countries (and globally) in order to meet commitments in the Paris Agreement to reduce emissions, taking into account domestic circumstances and capabilities.

Source: UNFCCC (2020[4]).

These growing needs lead governments to consider green budget tagging as a tool to help mobilise change. However, tagging is not the only tool which can help integrate green considerations into the budget processes and improve transparency and accountability on how money is being spent. It is important to consider the merits of tagging alongside policy measures such as regulations and providing linkages between expenditure and results to feed into the policy process and decision making – otherwise, tagging runs the risk of expenditure bias, where greater attention is placed on spending and investment than on the solution (World Bank, forthcoming[2]). There have been efforts to monitor programmes in relation to impacts on various dimensions including poverty, seen in the World Bank's Public Expenditure Reviews, as well as the environment, seen in the United Kingdom's *Green Book* (Pradhan, 1996[5]; HM Treasury,

2018[6]), further illustrated in Box 3. In other instances, tools such as the Climate Public Expenditure and Institutional Reviews (CPEIRs) have been a useful diagnostic tool for many countries in assessing opportunities and constraints for integrating climate change concerns within the budget allocation and expenditure process. These provide a qualitative and quantitative analysis of a country's public expenditures and how they relate to climate change, its climate change plans and policies, institutional framework, and public finance architecture (World Bank, 2014[7]; UNDP, 2019[8]). Before embarking on tagging, undertaking an exercise such as this can help countries take stock of their existing climate change structures and resources, and serve as a baseline for designing further reforms. For many countries, particularly in Asia, CPEIRs have been instrumental for starting the design for country-level tagging processes.

Box 3. The *Green Book* in the United Kingdom

In the United Kingdom, the *Green Book* is issued by HM Treasury and provides information on how to appraise policies, programmes and projects by providing guidance on the design and use of monitoring and evaluation before and after implementation. This ranges from policy and programme development, taxation and benefit proposals tochanges to existing public assets and resources. In particular, it provides an integrated approach to the assessment of climate mitigation, transition and other sustainability considerations across all government programmes.

Source: HM Treasury (2018[6]).

Additionally, it is important to identify tagging in relation to specific country contexts. In countries that already have practices in place to identify the environmental impacts of policy measures, the value added of tagging practices may be limited. For instance, in Switzerland, it is mandatory to analyse the environmental and economic effects of new policy propositions. As this allows an identification of the environmental effects of many budget measures, including subsidies and tax expenditures which may have big impacts, tagging efforts may provide limited benefits. However, in contexts where there is limited environmental assessment with little to no transparency on the budget, tagging efforts can provide significant added value in helping a country address its green objectives.

This sort of "first principle" work helps ensure that governments are clear on the purpose of green budgeting and its associated tools, such as green budget tagging, before implementing them. The best results from green budget tagging emerge when its design and implementation fulfil a need that emerges from government strategy or policy. Having a clear purpose helps communicate to internal government stakeholders why the practice is being introduced. It also helps inform the design of these tools.

The main benefits of implementing a tagging system include raising awareness, giving visibility to government action, mobilising resources, and improving the monitoring and reporting of climate change policies and international climate commitments (UNDP, 2019[8]). Compared to other methods for assessing how budgets align with green objectives, institutionalised domestic budget tagging has the advantage of being more sustainable and better integrated in budgeting processes. Where tags are integrated in financial management systems, real-time tracking of actual expenditures is enabled (World Bank, forthcoming[2]).

1.2. Designing an approach to green budget tagging

While there are significant differences in country contexts and public financial management systems, there are also common decisions that must be taken in designing any approach to green budget tagging. This includes: defining what is "green", deciding what budget measures to tag and developing a classifications system that is fit for purpose. Countries must also decide what type of information is needed from the tagging process. This helps to inform the design of the weighting system in order to capture the proportion that is relevant, depending on institutional capacity and the need for an accurate measure of relevant budget items. This section provides guidance on how to approach each of these key decisions.

Figure 1. Key decisions in designing an approach to green budget tagging

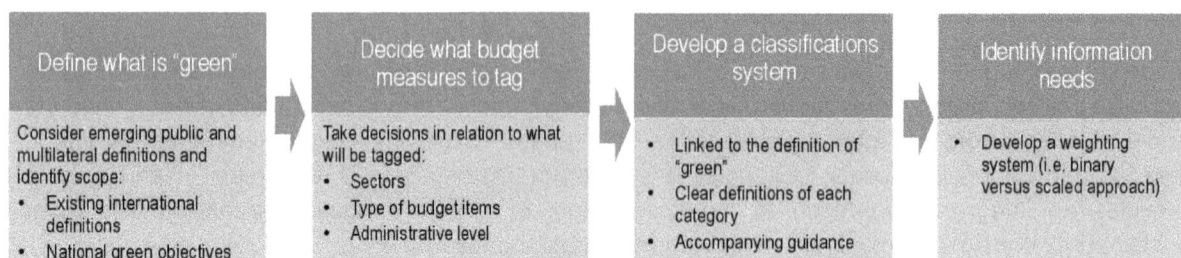

Define what is "green"	Decide what budget measures to tag	Develop a classifications system	Identify information needs
Consider emerging public and multilateral definitions and identify scope: • Existing international definitions • National green objectives	Take decisions in relation to what will be tagged: • Sectors • Type of budget items • Administrative level	• Linked to the definition of "green" • Clear definitions of each category • Accompanying guidance	• Develop a weighting system (i.e. binary versus scaled approach)

1.2.1. Defining what is "green"

Defining "green" budget items is not a straightforward task given that there is no common international definition. At its essence, "green" budget items are those which have a positive contribution towards broad environmental objectives, whether it be objectives relating to mitigating or adapting to climate change, or those related to other environmental dimensions such as ecosystems, biodiversity, water management, air quality, protection of marine resources, pollution prevention, etc. This also includes consideration for the various shades of green, such as the degree to which the budget contributes positively or negatively to environmental impacts. As such, existing definitions of "green investment" vary – making the purpose of an investment critical to defining the green criteria (Inderst, Kaminker and Stewart, 2012[9]).

"Green" budget tagging is invariably conflated with climate budget tagging. While climate budget tagging, similar to other tagging practices such as biodiversity tagging, is a subset of green budget tagging, these practices focus specifically on tagging budget items relevant to a narrower range of environmental goals. Green budget tagging may also have a wider purview relating to a number of environmental goals. It may indeed be that green budget tagging starts off tagging budget items related to a narrower range of environmental goals, then these practices provide useful foundations for building on tagging relating to other environmental objectives.

Invariably, the definition of "green" that is used by any country for budget tagging depends on the national country context. The decision is likely to be influenced by the scope of national green objectives. The choice will also depend on the purpose and ambition for green budget tagging in each country, as well as capacity. In developing the definition of "green" to be used for tagging, countries may also wish to – and have in the past – draw on existing definitions used by different international bodies (such as those in Box 4). Using existing definitions of "green" has the added benefit of facilitating international comparability.

Box 4. Definitions of "green" used by international organisations

European Union (EU) Taxonomy for Sustainable Finance: The EU Taxonomy defines investments in economic activities which make a substantial contribution to one of six environmental objectives: 1) climate change mitigation; 2) climate change adaptation; 3) sustainable use and protection of fresh water and marine resources; 4) transition to a circular economy; 5) pollution prevention and control; and 6) protection and restoration of biodiversity and ecosystems, without harming any of the other activities.

Joint MDB definition of climate finance: Refers to the financial resources (own-account and managed by multilateral development banks, MDBs) committed by MDBs to development operations and components which enable activities that mitigate climate and support adaptation to climate change in developing and emerging economies.

International Capital Markets Association (ICMA) green bonds: The Green Bond Principles explicitly recognise several broad categories of eligibility for investments in green projects, which contribute to the following environmental objectives: climate change mitigation, climate change adaptation, natural resource conservation, biodiversity conservation, and pollution prevention and control. Several states have issued sovereign green bonds and green bond frameworks to define the scope of their green investment with the bonds' proceeds (Belgium, Fiji, France, the Netherlands, etc.).

OECD-DAC Rio markers: Four Rio markers – biodiversity, climate change mitigation, climate change adaptation and desertification – are used to monitor aid targeting environmental sustainability in general and the objectives of the Rio Conventions in particular.

Sources: European Commission (2018[10]); AfDB et al. (2015[11]); ICMA (2018[12]); OECD (2016[13]).

As countries set out a definition of "green", it is important to consider linkages to existing principles, standards and metrics at the international level. As later noted in Section 2.7, this includes finding ways to align efforts to existing international statistical standards (such as the Classification of Environmental Activities, CEA). This can help give credibility to national approaches and facilitates cross-country comparisons and analysis.

Once "green" has been defined at the national level, the task of tagging can still be complex for several reasons:

- A number of different operational definitions of "green" may be in place across government, thus the relevant definition needs to be clearly communicated so that it is widely understood and not confused with others.

- There can be a sizeable common intersection of the various definitions in terms of some budget items (e.g. renewable energy), commodities (e.g. carbon or renewable energy credits), services (e.g. waste management) and technologies (e.g. to enhance energy efficiency).

- Defining "greenness" is easier for some budget items than for others, e.g. those with multiple purposes, some of which are green and others not (such as adaptation spending which serves to address the consequences of environmental change induced by human action). There are also some areas where data are difficult to obtain as well as areas where there can be disagreement (e.g. nuclear and large-scale hydro energy), changing consensus (e.g. biofuels, biomass, shale gas), ambiguity (e.g. agriculture, green IT, financial services, waste) or uncertainty how to deal with (e.g. biodiversity, conservation) (Inderst, Kaminker and Stewart, 2012[9]).

- Depending on a country's green commitments and climate objectives (such as the NDCs), the "greenness" of a budget item can be characterised in absolute terms (a budget item is green or not green) or in relative terms (e.g. one budget item has lower greenhouse gas emissions than another or is more energy-efficient).

- Definitions of "green" can be based on *ex ante* arguments (e.g. any activity in sustainable energy, energy efficiency or water management) or on specific indicators. There are qualitative and quantitative definitions, trying to measure different grades of "greenness". Quantitative definitions require some sort of indicator or measure of greenness (e.g. greenhouse gas emissions, energy efficiency, recycling and waste management, more points in a scoring system, etc.). In other instances, as seen in the EU Taxonomy for Sustainable Finance, a "do no harm" principle is put in place to ensure that the pursuit of one of the six environmental objectives does not harm any of the other five objectives.

For these reasons, it is important to set out, alongside the definition of "green", clear guidance that defines the boundaries of the tagging, and explains how to tag in these more complex circumstances. For instance, some objectives may positively contribute to some objectives (i.e. climate change adaptation), but may potentially negatively affect others (i.e. biodiversity). Understanding the purpose of the budget item is key in order to pin green criteria down, as it allows for the navigation of potential conflicts.

1.2.2. Deciding what budget measures to tag

Green budget tagging can cover different elements of the budget. There are a range of coverage issues, including the breadth of sectors and budget coverage, the type of budget items to include (positive or negative impact, revenue, expenditure, and different types of expenditure) and the administrative level of tagging (central government, subnational government, state-owned enterprises).

In terms of the breadth of budget coverage, green budget tagging should as a minimum aim to cover budget measures in priority sectors such as agriculture, transport, energy, industry and the environment, where budget measures tend to have significant impacts on climate and environmental objectives. Where budget classification is not by sector but by expenditure type, priority may be given to those expenditure areas most likely to have strong impacts on green objectives. However, as budget measures across all government areas can have a significant impact on climate change and environment objectives, countries should work towards covering budget measures across all sectors and expenditure types where capacity allows and where they are relevant according to their environmental objectives and pathways.

In terms of the type of budget items to include, countries should aim for green budget tagging to include both positive and negative measures. Country practices until now tend to only identify positive expenditure while other items such as negative expenditure, revenues, tax expenditures and subsidies – which are often more politically sensitive – are excluded (World Bank, forthcoming[2]). In some instances, this is likely to be related to the political sensitivity of negative measures, but it is also likely to be related to capacity considerations. For instance, there may be public support for fuel subsidies or pressure from interest groups (i.e. fossil fuel lobby) or limited capacity to fully identify and analyse an activity's carbon footprint. In other instances, areas which have a negative impact towards the environment and climate can conflict with pro-social policies, such as winter-fuel subsidies for low-income households. As elaborated in Section 4.5, information on negative expenditures can help kick-start policy discussions on the environmental as well as associated social and economic trade-offs of different budget items. This can be important as tagging can help to identify these tensions, allowing policy makers to develop more coherent and well-designed measures across multiple policy dimensions.

The exclusion of negative measures is problematic, as analysis in Finland and Indonesia has shown that they may outweigh positive measures. Reducing harmful measures is a key feature of climate and environmental policy and should go hand in hand with increased positive measures (World Bank, forthcoming[2]). To overcome this, countries can phase their approach to tagging and start with capturing positive expenditures, then subsequently expand the practice to include negative (brown) expenditures as greater capacity is developed within the Ministry of Finance and line ministries, as in the case of Ireland. Some countries also make efforts to identify these items as part of a separate exercise (see Box 5 for some examples).

Box 5. Examples of efforts to identify environmentally harmful spending and tax expenditures

Germany: The German Federal Environment Agency has published a series of reports on environmentally harmful subsidies. The reports are structured around a sectoral approach identifying environmentally harmful subsidies in four main sectors: 1) energy supply and use; 2) transport; 3) construction and housing; and 4) agriculture, forestry and fisheries.

Italy: The Italian Catalogue of Environmentally Friendly and Harmful Subsidies was developed by the Ministry of Environment, Land and Sea in response to a request by the Italian parliament, as part of a general effort aiming to analyse and evaluate fiscal erosion due to tax breaks and tax expenditures. The catalogue analyses the subsidies by sector: agriculture, energy, transport, value-added tax and other subsidies, considering both direct subsidies and tax expenditures.

Sources: Umweltbundesamt (2016[14]), Italian Ministry of Environment, Land and Sea (2017[15]).

A further issue is whether tagging covers the full range of expenditures, including recurrent and investment/development budgets. As countries consider the scope of tagging, the exclusion of recurrent budgets such as civil servant salaries may potentially underestimate the amount of relevant green expenditures. As these overheads can be a vital part of investment and development budgets, arguments can be made to ensure they are included. Where tagging is applied to budget programmes rather than line items, both recurrent and investment budgets will be covered. Other expenditures such as in the area of the procurement of goods and services can be assessed in relation to use of green procurement practices through the use of relevant specifications and criteria (OECD, 2019[16]).

A final consideration on the scope of tagging is whether or not to include subnational budget measures. In this regard, it is worth bearing in mind that the case for tagging to cover local government budgets is particularly strong where there are high levels of fiscal decentralisation and where tax and spending in areas relevant to climate and environmental policy are devolved. Because subnational governments play a critical role in land-use management, urban services, transport, water and environmental management functions, many governments have applied tagging methodologies to transfers to sub-government expenditures (World Bank, forthcoming[2]). Furthermore, although not currently common practice, there is an argument for tagging to cover the budgets of state-owned enterprises where they account for an important share of government expenditures and play an important role role in environmentally relevant sectors (such as energy, water and transport).

With these considerations, it is important to identify the relative costs and benefits of a fully comprehensive tagging approach. A fully comprehensive approach may provide added value but may require significant costs in time, training and resources. On the other hand, a less comprehensive approach may incur fewer resource costs but may not provide sufficient added value to achieve its intended purpose.

1.2.3. Developing a classifications system

Once the definition of "green" in the country context and with the scope of tagging have been decided, a classifications system can be identified or developed that helps to ensure that the tagging system gathers the right information. Different types of classifications systems are highlighted in Table 1.

Table 1. Classifications systems for green budget tagging across select countries

Approach	Country	Purpose of green budget tagging	Classification system
Focused on identifying climate-relevant budget items	Bangladesh	Climate budget tagging helps the country to track and report climate finance.	Expenditures are tagged if they contribute to one of the 6 thematic areas (food security/social protection/health, comprehensive disaster management, infrastructure, research and knowledge management, mitigation and low-carbon development, capacity building and institutional strengthening) or one of the 44 programmes under the national climate change policy.
	Colombia	Climate budget tagging aims to help achieve the country's goals as part of the United Nations Framework Convention on Climate Change.	Tagging covers national, regional and local expenditures along 12 sectors considered the most directly linked to mitigation and adaptation efforts.
	Ireland	Green budget tagging supports the reporting requirements relating to Irish sovereign green bonds.	Tagging identifies expenditure that is dedicated to addressing climate change (using the International Capital Market Association's standard definition of "green expenditure").
Focused on identifying budget items relevant to climate and other environmental dimensions	France	Green budget tagging helps improve transparency around government policy relating to the environment and climate change and aims to improve decision making on public policies.	Budget items are classified using the six different categories defined in the EU Taxonomy for Sustainable Finance: climate change adaptation, mitigation, biodiversity, circular economy, water management and air quality.
	Italy	Green budget tagging was introduced at the request of parliament for improved transparency on environmental expenditure.	Tagging identifies expenditure items in accordance with the classifications system set out in the European System for the Collection of Economic Information on the Environment (SERIEE) addressing environmental protection and reducing environmental degradation.
	Philippines	Climate budget tagging was introduced to help track how much expenditure is going towards the priority areas set out in the country's National Climate Change Action Plan.	Tagging identifies expenditure across seven areas: food security, water sufficiency, ecosystem and environmental and ecological stability, human security, climate-smart industries and services, sustainable energy, and knowledge and capacity development.

Sources: OECD (forthcoming[17]); UNDP (2019[8]); World Bank (forthcoming[2]); Climate Change Commission (2019[18]); Climate Change Commission (n.d.[19]); Ministry of the Ecological Transition (2020[20]); Cremins and Kevany (2018[21]).

For definitions of "green" that focus on climate change, often referred to as "climate budget tagging" or "climate expenditure tagging", countries may use one category for climate-relevant items (as in the case of Ireland) or break it down between adaptation and mitigation (as is the case in countries such as Bangladesh), depending on the extent to which detailed information is needed. Many countries follow the OECD-DAC Rio marker definitions for activities which contribute to climate adaptation and mitigation (Box 6) (OECD, 2016[13]).

Where definitions of "green" include environmental activities beyond climate mitigation or adaptation, such as air and water management quality, and biodiversity, classifications may be guided by or aligned with national strategies in the area of climate and the environment. For example, in Honduras, tagging includes climate-related disaster management, which covers activities related to reducing the impact of natural hazards and environmental disasters (World Bank, forthcoming[2]). In Bangladesh and Kyrgyzstan, tagging also includes identifying programmes contributing to biodiversity and conservation. Existing usages of these definitions can be found in Box 7.

To help facilitate the classifications process, it is useful to provide clear definitions of the type of budget items that qualify under each category of objectives. The definitions should be sufficiently broad to reflect the cross-sectoral nature of climate and environmental policy, yet sufficiently narrow to be meaningful and credible (World Bank, forthcoming[2]). The cross-cutting nature of climate and environmental policy also means that budget measures may qualify to be tagged in more than one category. Tagging guidance should thus also be clear on what to do in this instance (e.g. only tagging budget measures which directly address each objective). Some countries develop a "positive" and "negative" list of indicative investments to help guide classification (consideration of "negative" expenditures is further detailed in Section 4.3). For example, Colombia's methodological guide to climate budget tagging includes an annex that provides an indicative list of activities by sector and subsector that qualify as climate mitigation or climate adaptation (Government of Colombia, 2016[27]).

As countries work to develop their classification process, close co-ordination with the national statistical office can help harmonise approaches to existing international classification standards. This can mean working to co-develop an approach that helps address a country's "green" objectives that allows statistical offices (or other agencies managing national accounts) to concurrently use the information to facilitate reporting against global statistical standards. Further considerations in relation to this "statistical tagging" approach are further detailed in Section 2.7.

As countries engage in this process, country experiences have highlighted key challenges for consideration (further highlighted in Section 4). This includes identifying the appropriate level of granularity for tagging, deciding how to address budget measures related to adaptation and disaster risk management, negative expenditures, ensuring consistency and quality as well as balancing environmental objectives with social and economic objectives.

1.2.4. Identify information needs: Developing a weighting system

Another important design choice for any green budget tagging practice is to identify information needed for the purpose of data tagging. This provides inputs into the development of an appropriate weighting system for budget items. For instance, if a country decides to only track those expenditures that mostly contribute towards green objectives, as in the case of Ireland, it can adopt a more binary approach (either budget programme is tagged or not). On the other hand, if a country decides to track the extent to which all of its expenditures contribute to its green objectives, it can adopt a more scaled approach in order to identify the proportion of expenditures attributed to the objectives.

The weighting system determines the share of the tagged budget item that is considered (and counted) as green. In most cases, relevant expenditures are costed out on an input basis (as used in methodologies by many multilateral development banks) or identified proportionately, where the amount allocated to a specific objective is proportional to the relevance of the expenditure. Examples of countries employing a costed methodology are Indonesia, where tags are placed on outputs and sub-programmes, as well as Nicaragua and Uganda, where tags are placed on the activity level and sub-programme level respectively.

Countries employing a weighting system often try to identify expenditures proportionately by either categorising those that have a primary purpose related to green objectives, often seen in binary approaches, or through a scaled approach where attempts are made to estimate the co-benefits or the degree of climate relevance of a budgetary programme. For instance, when it comes to expenditure on urban transport, only the share of expenditure that has co-benefits with climate change mitigation (by reducing GHG emissions per unit transported) is tagged. In other instances, countries have further assigned weights to expenditures that have been identified as having co-benefits to green objectives. There are two main approaches when it comes to weighting and green budget tagging: the binary approach and the scaled approach.

Under a binary approach, either the full cost of a budget item is tagged or none is. For example, research and development (R&D) expenditure would either be fully included or not included at all, even if it is the case that just a portion of the expenditure relates to the stated objectives. While this can be simpler than the scaled approach and may serve the needs of a particular tagging exercise or be useful as a first step in budget tagging, it provides a less accurate picture of the quantity of revenues and expenditure that are relevant. Countries pursuing a binary approach to weighting may find it helpful to employ a more conservative tagging approach. This means only counting those budget items which are significantly relevant to the national climate and environmental agendas. A notable example of this is in Ireland, where tagging only includes expenditure items which "significantly contribute" towards lowering GHG emissions. This conservative approach can ensure that a binary system does not give an overestimation of the figures, withstanding accusations of "greenwashing" by stakeholders. However, as it excludes expenditure items which may have medium and low relevance to national climate objectives, the tagging may not capture the full breadth of relevant budget items.

A scaled weighting system allows for a certain proportion of a budget item to be tagged. Often, budget items will include some revenue or expenditure that is relevant for the tagging exercise and some that is not (as was the case with the R&D expenditure illustration above). The calculation of the proportion of the budget item that is relevant may be based on either an inputs or outputs approach. An inputs approach is simpler and considers the proportion of the budget measure that is relevant to green objectives, while an outputs approach considers the proportion of the outputs associated with the budget measure that are relevant to green objectives. The outputs approach is inevitably open to a greater degree of subjectivity.

Most countries that currently undertake green budget tagging employ a scaled approach to weighting since it allows a more granular quantification of relevant revenues and expenditure. This means budget items are categorised in accordance to their degree of relevance to green objectives. For revenues and expenditure where the primary purpose is not specifically climate change adaptation, for example, only the share with co-benefits to adaptation is tagged. In many cases, approaches are based on the OECD-DAC Rio marker methodology, shown in Box 8.

Box 8. OECD-DAC Rio marker methodology for budget tagging

The OECD-DAC Rio markers have served as a reference for OECD Development Assistance Committee (DAC) donors to tag bilateral aid projects along four thematic areas: biodiversity, desertification control, climate mitigation and climate adaptation. The Rio markers employ a three-step classification system:

- "**not targeted**": an activity is not targeted to policy objective (e.g. roads)
- "**significant**": an activity which contributes to but does not primarily address policy objective (e.g. air quality measures)
- "**principal**": an activity which the policy objective is the explicit objective (e.g. wind farms).

Countries build on the Rio marker methodology by adapting them to their classification and weighting approach. In certain instances, when expenditures are weighted, countries have assigned percentages along the three categories to identify the degree to which an activity or expenditure contributes to its degree of relevance. For instance, in Ghana, whose approach is influenced by the Rio markers, expenditure items are tagged along high relevance (100%), medium relevance (50%) and low relevance (20%). In the European Union, items are tagged and weighted as "not targeted" (0%), "significant" (40%) and "principle" (100%).

Sources: OECD (2011[28]); Petri (2017[29]); World Bank (forthcoming[2]); UNDP (2019[8]).

A scaled approach may be simple, or complex. A simple scaled approach, such as the OECD-DAC Rio markers, sets out considerations for identifying different weights to budget items. This type of approach is relatively easy to implement and is more accurate than binary weighting. A complex scaled approach, as seen in Bangladesh, builds on this by factoring in counterfactuals to the weighting process (as further illustrated in Box 8). This approach entails using modules to further narrow down the degree of relevance with which budget items are classified beyond categorical degrees seen in more simplified approaches (e.g. highly relevant, relevant, neutral). The complex scaled approach gives the potential for the most granular information among the different weighting systems, but requires greater capacity for analysis and builds on assumptions which may result in errors in overestimating or underestimating its relationship to climate change or the environment. This represents a benefits-based approach where it works to assess the proportion of total programme benefits associated with a green objective, as seen in Bangladesh. Examples of countries that use each of these different weighting systems are provided in Box 9.

Box 9. Country examples of the different approaches

Ireland (binary): Ireland adopted a conservative classification approach where it only tagged programmes where it is evident that all, or at least the majority of, investment in question supports Ireland's transition to a low-carbon, climate-resilient and environmentally sustainable economy.

Moldova (scaled – simplified): Programmes, activities and projects which mainly address climate change are fully counted with a 100% weight. Those that do not directly address climate change are classified and weighted in accordance to four categories:

- high relevance with a 70% weight (more than 65% of activities dedicated to climate-related interventions
- medium relevance with a 50% weight (40-65% of activities)
- neutral relevance with a 25% weight (14-40% of activities)
- marginal relevance (less than 15% of activities or with very indirect and theoretical links) are not counted.

France (scaled – simplified): Expenditures were tagged in accordance to their impact towards six objectives (climate change mitigation, climate change adaptation [and natural risk prevention], water resource management, the circular economy, pollution abatement, and biodiversity and sustainable land use):

- favourable: directly targeted environmental expenses
- favourable (indirect): no explicit environmental target, but indirect positive impact
- favourable but controversial: e.g. short-term favourable effects but presence of a long-term technology lock-in risk
- neutral: no significant or no information
- unfavourable: environmentally harmful expenditure.

Nepal (scaled – simplified): Activities relevant to its list of 11 climate change-related activities are classified (not weighted) into three categories:

- highly relevant (more than 60% of the programme budget allocated to climate activities)
- relevant (20-60% of the budget)
- neutral (less than 20% of the budget).

Bangladesh (scaled – complex): Applies a climate-relevant weight to all relevant expenditures. Weights are calculated by identifying the difference between the degrees of relevance (%) an expenditure area has towards climate change with the share of expenditure (%) which would still take place in the absence of climate change.

- *Example:* The development of seed production, storage and supply systems is considered 100% relevant. In the absence of climate change, 40% of the expenditure would still take place.

  Thus, the weighting is calculated as:

  [Weight Score] = [100%] – [40%] = 60% weight

Sources: Cremins and Kevany (2018[21]); Ministry of Ecological Transition (2020[20]); World Bank (forthcoming[2]); UNDP (2019[8]).

1.3. Deciding which stage of the budget process to cover

Green budget tagging may be undertaken at the *ex ante* phase of the budget (tagging planned allocations before the budget is approved and executed) or the *ex post* phase (an evaluation of expenditures after the budget has been executed). Undertaking the tagging exercise *ex ante* can theoretically provide useful evidence to help frame budget and policy decisions as they are being formulated. However, typically, programmes and projects are tagged after they have been approved, too late to inform the design of the budget (although they can still inform the following budget cycle), rationalising rather than informing resource allocation (World Bank, forthcoming[2]). The scope for tagging to make significant impact on resource allocation is the greatest where tags are applied before measures have been planned and budgeted. Information may also be presented in reports accompanying the draft budget and supporting parliamentary oversight. In the Philippines, the tagging is applied during the budget preparation; then updated after budget hearings, once the proposed budget is developed to the Congress; and finally, once Congress has approved the budget. This allows the information to be taken into account in budget preparation, but also ensures that any changes to the budget emanating from budget hearings or legislative review are reflected (UNDP, 2019[8]).

Green budget tagging may also be done on an *ex post* basis. *Ex post* tagging provides a more accurate picture of how the budget was used, after budget execution. From an accountability perspective, there are strong benefits of doing both *ex ante* and *ex post* reporting, as it allows oversight of how the government intends to use the budget, and also whether or not the government actually allocated resources in the way it had planned. This is further illustrated in Figure 2. It also allows scope for policy learning and adaptive governance, which is associated with more successful tagging systems (Resch et al., 2017[30]). At present, most countries undertake green budget tagging at the *ex ante* phase of the budget process. However, Italy is an example of a country that does budget tagging at both the *ex ante* and *ex post* phases.

When considering *ex post* evaluations, it is important to consider that it is difficult to obtain a global view of the environmental impact of budget measures when only a selected set of tagged budget items are assessed. France, for example, conducts systematic environmental assessments of all budget actions in coherence with the recommendations from the independent High Council for Climate (*Haut Conseil pour le Climat*) (Haut Conseil pour le Climat, 2019[31]). Another example can be seen in Sweden with the established Climate Policy Council evaluating how government policies address the country's climate objectives (Swedish Ministry of the Environment and Energy, 2018[32]).

2. Implementing green budget tagging

Once the approach to green budgeting has been defined, the next challenge for governments is to think about how it can be successfully implemented. This means ensuring that the tagging approach is sequenced in a manner where it addresses its intended objective with consideration of the roles, responsibilities and capacity of stakeholders and internal systems, processes to ensure the quality of the information, and linkages to existing standards. The following sections cover some of the key considerations, including how green budget tagging fits within a broader approach to green budgeting, the roles and responsibilities of different stakeholders in implementing the tagging, the sequencing of implementation, how to build up capacity and expertise among civil servants, and ensuring that the internal systems are fit for purpose. Governments will also wish to consider how to develop a quality assurance process to ensure rigorous, consistent and coherent tagging and how they can build a bridge between budget tagging and statistical tagging, which allows international comparisons on finance flows.

2.1. Ensuring there is a strong strategic framework to guide tagging

Green budget tagging can be particularly effective where it is part of a wider approach to green budgeting that is guided by a strong strategic framework (see Figure 2). A strategic framework refers to relevant strategies, policies and plans which include clear goals for government policy, as set out in the OECD's Green Budgeting Framework. For example, in Nepal and Pakistan, the development of a Climate Change Financing Framework has been vital to promote a more integrated approach to facilitate climate finance reforms (Pakistani Controller General of Accounts, 2020[33]; Nepalese Ministry of Agriculture, 2020[34]). Experiences from tagging practices preceding green budget tagging show that the strategic framework needs to be specific enough to guide budget allocations, including realistic cost estimates and an operational framework (World Bank, forthcoming[2]). In this way, green budget tagging can be used to help direct resources towards the strategic priorities of government in the areas of climate and the environment. A well-defined strategic framework can also help guide what budget items are relevant for tagging, particularly in more ambiguous situations. For example, a combined cycle power plant replacing a carbon power plant may be considered to be climate-positive relative to the status quo, but also climate-negative since natural gas still contributes to global warming. Understanding the extent to which the development aligns with longer term climate policy helps in developing guidance for how to define such items.

Figure 2. OECD Green Budgeting Framework

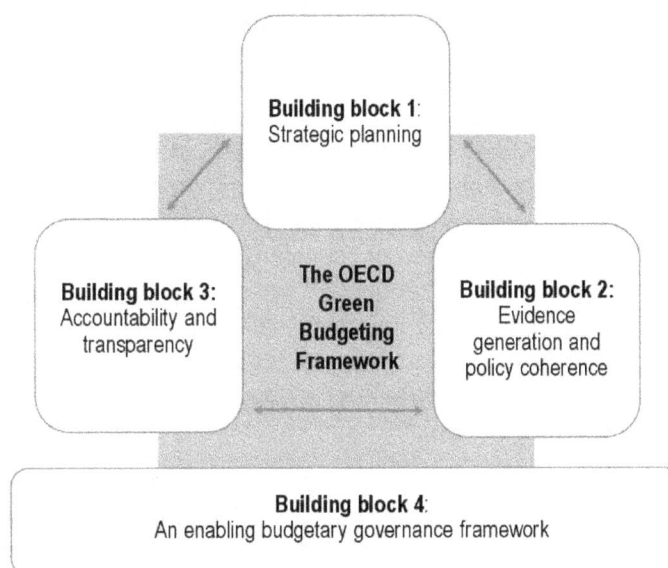

Building block 1:
Strategic planning

Building block 3:
Accountability and
transparency

**The OECD
Green
Budgeting
Framework**

Building block 2:
Evidence
generation and
policy coherence

Building block 4:
An enabling budgetary governance framework

Source: OECD (2020[1]).

2.2. Setting out the roles and responsibilities of different stakeholders

Identifying the roles and responsibilities of different stakeholders is an important element to implementing green budget tagging. The central budget authority (CBA) and Ministry of the Environment or Climate Change have important leadership roles. As part of the leadership role of these institutions, clear responsibilities for the different actors involved (including line ministries, the national statistical office and citizens) should be set out.

2.2.1. Developing a whole-of-government approach

The CBA has a central leadership role in relation to green budgeting and "the power of the purse" means that it usually has considerable ability to drive its implementation.[2] A particularly important partner is the Ministry of the Environment or Climate Change. The CBA often works hand-in-hand with the Ministry of the Environment or Climate Change counterparts in leading the implementation of green budget tagging. In Kenya, for example, close engagement between the Ministry of Finance and the climate change policy body has helped to lead the implementation of climate budget tagging and for it to become embedded in the country's policy and legal frameworks (UNDP, 2019[8]). In Pakistan, the Controller General of Accounts and the Ministry of Climate Change worked together to configure the internal system to assign weights to mitigation and adaptation-related expenditures as well as including climate change into the medium-term budgetary framework in two line ministries (Pakistani Controller General of Accounts, 2020[33]).

Embedding practices such as green budget tagging often also requires the collective effort of wider government stakeholders. A key consideration is who has primary responsibility for tagging different budget items. Some countries have centralised tagging processes, where tagging is predominantly undertaken by the CBA, or the Ministry of the Environment or Climate Change; others have a more decentralised model where tagging is the responsibility of individual line ministries. Each approach has its own merits.

Centralised tagging processes can allow for more consistent tagging, and also have the benefit of being easier to introduce given it involves fewer stakeholders. In France, for example, tagging is conducted by a limited but dedicated team of people within the Ministry for the Ecological Transition (Ministère de la Transition écologique) and the Ministry for the Economy and Finance who tag relevant budget lines to their six areas of classification. In Bangladesh, a special unit within the Ministry of Finance reviews line ministry budget frameworks and annual development programmes in accordance to their relevance to climate objectives.

Decentralised tagging approaches involve the active participation of line ministries in tagging their budget measures. Where line ministries play a leading role in the tagging process, this may be co-ordinated either by the budget unit or in conjunction with relevant technical staff and co-ordinated at the government level by the CBA and the Ministry of the Environment or Climate Change, who aggregate, reconcile and verify information. This is the more common form of tagging across countries. In Indonesia, for example, specific units ("Echelon II units/directorates") within line ministries are responsible for tagging budgets for submission to the Ministry of Finance. Through a formal reconciliation period of the budgeting process, line ministries meet with the Ministry of Finance to address questions and make adjustments to the tagged budget of outputs (World Bank, forthcoming[2]).

Although decentralised approaches involve more stakeholders, this whole-of-government approach can help build collective ownership of the tagging exercise, and engenders greater awareness of climate and environmental objectives, which can help integrate green perspectives into the policy development process. Furthermore, giving responsibilities to the line ministries also helps to ensure that the tagging is conducted by those who are the most attuned to the nature of ministry programmes. However, there is a risk that some may "greenwash" budget items as a means to game budget negotiations or minimise negative perceptions of their programmes in relation to green objectives. In other instances, due to a lack of verification procedures and heterogeneous approaches, there can be overestimations, as seen in the use of the Rio markers (Weikmans et al., 2017[35]). Because of these inherent incentives, it is important to include validation checks to minimise instances of gaming by ministries and agencies. In addition, decentralised tagging requires a sufficient level of capacity within the government both in terms of training for ministry staff and support systems (e.g. IT systems), and relies on the compliance of a much larger group of stakeholders. Tagging systems that overstretch human resources are unlikely to be sustained.

2.2.2. Strong collaboration and co-ordination mechanisms

In many instances, strong collaboration between institutions is observed in the development and implementation of green budget tagging. This collaboration may be witnessed in the adoption of a joint approach to leading the reform initiative and setting out guidance for tagging. For example, in the Philippines, after a Climate Public Expenditure and Institutional Review (CPEIR), the Department for Management and Budget conducted consultations with agencies to gather inputs to inform the development of the typology and guidance within the joint memorandum circular (Crepin, 2013[36]). In another example, in Colombia, the National Planning Department and the Financial Management Committee of the National Climate System worked together to develop the country's tagging methodology. At times, however, failure to identify institutional partners in the development of the tagging process may impede efforts over time. In the same example in Colombia, the Ministry of Finance and line ministries were not involved in the development of the tagging methodology, leading to an underlying lack of clarity about the division of labour between entities as well as an overall lack of ownership for the results (World Bank, forthcoming[2]).

Additionally, strong co-ordination mechanisms (for example, an inter-agency working group) can potentially be a valuable element of any ongoing approach to green budgeting since it involves different stakeholders from across government (in some cases also including subnational governments). This facilitates a consistent approach, as well as exchange of good practices among different stakeholders. Inter-agency working groups can also help to address resistance to new processes by ensuring that the needs of different stakeholders are communicated across government. These working groups are often seen supporting the implementation of similar practices such as gender budgeting (see Box 10 for the example of Nepal). It is, however, important to note that working groups often require a significant time commitment, largely due to challenges co-ordinating with multiple government stakeholders. As such, it is important to ensure groups are only comprised of essential stakeholders, and that they have a clear mandate and time frame for delivering their objectives.

Box 10. Nepal's inter-institutional Climate Finance Working Group

In the course of designing the country's tagging methodology, an inter-institutional Climate Finance Working Group was set up comprised of representatives from the National Planning Commission; the Ministry of Finance; the Ministry of Environment, Science and Technology; the Ministry of Federal Affairs and Local Development; and the Ministry of Forestry and Soil Conservation. This helped to facilitate a process that is attuned to institutional contexts as well as promote shared ownership of the tagging exercise through the budgeting and planning process.

Sources: World Bank (forthcoming[2]); UNDP (2015[37]).

2.2.3. Bringing in external viewpoints

Budgeting is a unique "nexus" that brings together the various dimensions of public policy analysis and that determines where the money goes. However, approaches such as green budgeting can require environmental policy expertise that is not inherent in the CBA. It is important that this nexus is open to expert inputs and viewpoints that can bring this expertise. In certain instances, an expert advisory group could help in this regard, providing technical guidance for the tagging exercise or green budgeting more generally as well as playing a challenge function. By incorporating expert representatives from civil society, the group can serve as a channel for insights on the needs of citizens ensuring these voices are heard in the decision-making process. This is something that has also proved useful in the implementation of practices such as gender budgeting and equality budgeting. For example, Ireland benefits from the advice of an expert advisory group in its implementation of equality budgeting (Box 11).

In 2018, Ireland established an Equality Budget Expert Advisory Group to assist the roll-out of equality budgeting. The objectives of the group were to: provide constructive, critical feedback on the equality budgeting initiative; provide expert guidance and informed insights on the future direction and areas of focus for equality budgeting; promote a coherent, cross-governmental approach to equality budgeting; and identify existing strengths of the Irish policy-making system that can be leveraged in support of equality budgeting, along with potential shortcomings that need to be addressed.

The group drew on a range of independent perspectives to provide expert guidance and momentum to equality budgeting. Chaired by the Department of Public Expenditure and Reform, the panel included government officials from the Department of Justice and Equality, the Department of Finance, the Department of Employment Affairs and Social Protection, the Central Statistics Office, and the National Economic and Social Council as well as representatives from the Irish Human Rights and Equality Commission, civil society and independent experts, including a representative from the Economic and Social Research Institute and the National Women's Council of Ireland.

Source: OECD (2019[38]).

2.3. Ensuring the quality of green budget tagging

Whether green budget tagging is undertaken by the CBA, the Ministry of the Environment and Climate Change or line ministries, it is crucial that there is a quality assurance process that ensures the rigour, consistency and coherence of tagging and the data it generates. This has been identified as a key weakness of existing systems of green budget tagging. Many countries lack the appropriate checks to ensure quality assurance of the information generated from tagging exercises. In cases like the Philippines, as in most contexts, the burden is on the line ministries to validate tagging, while in others such as Ghana, no validation process is identified (World Bank, forthcoming[2]; UNDP, 2019[8]).

A strong quality assurance process will ensure that budget measures are appropriately classified and will help limit the risk of "greenwashing" or undertagging of the budget. In centralised approaches where the Ministry of Finance and the Ministry of the Environment or Climate Change take the lead in tagging, this means setting procedures for line ministries to validate the data by involving reconciliation processes, as previously noted in the case of Indonesia. In decentralised approaches, it means working closely with the Ministry of Finance and the Ministry of the Environment or Climate Change by embedding similar reconciliation procedures to limit instances of "gaming" and ensuring that the data submitted are of sufficient quality. However, these can only make an impact if there is sufficient capacity (in terms of dedication of staff time, technical capability and integrated IT systems) within ministries. Lessons from the Philippines show that just mandating quality assessment procedures does not necessarily mean overall improvements. Upon requiring ministries to submit quality assessment and review forms of tagged expenditures, line ministries decreased the number of expenditures tagged to commensurately cope with the increased workload (World Bank, forthcoming[2]).

2.4. Developing a road map for implementation

Implementing green budget tagging requires the development of a road map, outlining the planned stages of implementation including: design of the green budget tagging framework, development of guidance, training and development, and implementation of tagging, often with an increase of the scope of tagging over time. The speed of implementation is determined by factors such as the strength of political will and administrative leadership, as well as the capacity of government to implement a new reform. Regardless, the introduction of green budget tagging is likely a reform that will take a number of budget cycles to bed in.

2.4.1. The early years of green budget tagging

The early years of green budget tagging – as with any reform – can be particularly challenging. For example, tagging is often more time-consuming, as it needs to be done for all baseline budget measures, whereas in subsequent years only new budget items need to be tagged. It may also be that in the beginning, existing IT systems do not yet have tagging functionality. In addition, it is in these early years that the effectiveness of the approach is still being tested and refined. To help overcome this, some countries have adopted a centralised approach to tagging at the beginning, involving the line ministries more progressively over time. An example of this approach that many countries have taken is provided by Bangladesh (Box 12).

Box 12. Bangladesh's adaptive approach to implementing climate budget tagging

In Bangladesh, climate tagging was originally done by the Finance Division, using the analysis of line ministries' planning templates. With the introduction of the new budget classification system, and an integrated budget and accounting system in 2018, a new climate finance module has been embedded in the new system – adding a segment to capture data on budget allocation and expenditure against the Bangladesh Climate Change Strategy and Action Plan. Under the evolved tagging system, tagging is done by line ministries with initial support of the Finance Division.

Source: UNDP (2019[8]).

The benefit of this is that the leaders of the reform – the CBA and the Ministry of the Environment and Climate Change – do a lot of the heavy lifting to get the initiative off the ground. This allows line ministries to become more involved at a time when tagging is less onerous, and provides the opportunity to build a rigorous classification system and the necessary capacity across government and its systems over time. However, it is also important to consider that this approach can demand significant time and commitment from a small number of central staff who, in some instances, may have to tag thousands of budget items. This can further be a challenge when central staff do not hold detailed knowledge about the nature of the budget items enabling them to make accurate determinations of climate and environmental relevance. As such, it is important to ensure that even where there is a centralised approach, staff do still engage with line ministries at some level to verify the accuracy of tagged budget items and ensure the quality of green budget tagging, as outlined in Section 2.3.

2.4.2. Developing tagging guidance

When green budget tagging is being rolled out to line ministries, it is helpful for clear guidance to be provided within budget guidelines or circulars that are issued during the annual budget process. An example is provided by the guidance issued for climate budget tagging in the Philippines (Box 13).

For centralised tagging processes, as engagements with line ministries are more limited, guidance usually comes in the form of requests for verifying tagged expenditures and opportunities for reconciliation. In other instances where the tagging system is more automatic (relying more on the financial management information system), tagging processes may require guidance on modifications made to the financial management information system as it pertains to classification and weighting, as well as information for Ministry of Finance staff on the updated changes to the system (UNDP, 2019[8]).

Box 13. Climate budget tagging guidance issued to line ministries in the Philippines

In the Philippines, a Joint Memorandum Circular issued by the Department of Budget and Management and the Climate Change Commission provides the following guidance for climate budget tagging:

- **Step 1:** Identify projects/activities/programmes (P/A/Ps) with climate-related adaptation and mitigation expenditures. This requires assigning expenditures as either under adaptation, mitigation, both or neither in accordance with their definitions.

- **Step 2:** Determine the climate change component(s) within the P/A/Ps using climate change typologies. This requires comparing activities in accordance with the typology provided within the circular and identifying the appropriate code accordingly.

- **Step 3:** Specify the amount of tagged climate change component. Disaggregating the amounts by personnel services, maintenance and other operating services, financial expenses, and capital outlays.

- **Step 4:** Identify and tag in the Outline Submission of the Budget Proposal. Encoding the amount and identified codes to the Online Submission of Budget Proposals system.

Source: UNDP (2019[8]).

2.5. Building capacity across government

Many countries implementing green budget tagging have noted that the practice can only be rolled out as capacity is strengthened across government agencies. Thus, plans for implementation may need to be adjusted depending on levels of existing capacity. Taking into account the experiences of countries so far in implementing green budget tagging, several lessons can be learnt in relation to developing capacity across government.

First, training is most effective when it is tailored to the needs of each stakeholder. In each country, institutions have varying roles and responsibilities. The CBA, for instance, may play a more co-ordinating role while Ministries of the Environment and Climate Change may take a more technical leadership role. The CBA's role is made easier when there is a baseline of policy knowledge in the area of climate and the environment. Ministries of the Environment and Climate Change may also need support in developing more effective budget execution. Identifying the appropriate responsibilities and the skillsets required by staff across all of these ministries is an important consideration when designing training.

An additional complexity is that the capacity of different line ministries to undertake tagging varies, and so capacity development needs are also different. For example, lessons from workshops in Nepal to design climate budget tagging procedures highlighted the potential challenge that not all ministries are able to produce the same level of detail in their proposed programmes (UNDP, 2019[8]). In addition, the extent to which different ministries face competing demands, perhaps from other ongoing reforms, should be taken to account. These considerations have already been taken into account by some countries implementing green budget tagging, for example in Bangladesh, Nepal and Pakistan, where tagging started with key relevant ministries and expanded gradually to other line ministries over time.

A further issue is that some design choices require greater capacity development. For example, decentralised approaches require significant capacity building in line ministries with centralised approaches involving fewer parties to be trained. Recognising this, in the Philippines, the Climate Change Commission and the Department of Budget and Management temporarily set up a help desk to assist line ministries in the first years of implementation (Box 14) (UNDP, 2019[8]).

Box 14. The Philippines' climate change expenditures tagging help desk

To build capacity and improve readiness to undertake tagging processes across the Philippine government, the Department for Budget and Management and the Climate Change Commission set up a help desk for line ministry staff. The help desk guides ministries on how to: evaluate agency proposals for their climate change components using existing typology and processes, review and approve new typology proposals of the agencies, and prepare climate budget briefs and reports based on the result of the tagging process. Annual trainings are held for budget and planning units.

Source: Department of Budget and Management (2020[39]).

Maintaining sufficient levels of capacity across the civil service can be challenging in contexts with high staff turnover. Oftentimes, country experiences have shown that trained staff are in their post for a limited time, requiring trainings to be repeated regularly to ensure those in appropriate roles (across technical, financial and administrative cadres) are adequately equipped to manage their respective tagging processes. As such, capacity development efforts are unlikely to be one-off, but instead will require ongoing engagement with continuous learning and adaption. In Ghana, for example, this includes training permanent secretaries and ministerial heads in addition to operational staff. Building sufficient capacity and maintaining it over time helps to ensure the sustainability of green budget tagging.

2.6. Ensuring internal budget management systems are fit for purpose

Efforts to implement green budget tagging have involved close consideration of a country's internal budget management systems, and whether they have existing tagging functionality that can be adapted for these purposes. Many tagging systems rely on integrated financial management information systems, as these are designed with a view to helping ministries aggregate and associate budget information along existing programmatic structures. This can be important when working to integrate green budget tagging into the larger budget process as the tagging exercise, for example, may be one of multiple components of a ministry's procedures to develop its annual budget proposals.

Some countries may also wish to use their Chart of Accounts and may adapt it for this purpose by defining or adding a relevant section to enable tagging. For example, in Nicaragua, thematic tags are associated with a code in the Chart of Accounts. In other instances, countries have introduced detailed climate change codes in their financial management systems to track expenditures at the sector, sub-sector and activity level.[3] For example, Ecuador has a six-digit thematic code integrated into its electronic Integrated Financial Management System (e-SIGEF) classifying expenditure by activities (World Bank, forthcoming[2]). In Ghana, the use and development of coding systems for budget tagging has helped to ensure greater transparency and accountability across the budget.

The use, development and adaptation of these systems means that budget measures can be analysed and tracked throughout the budget cycle more easily and can help support a more efficient tagging process across ministries. For instance, in Bangladesh, once line ministries identify appropriate budget measures to be tagged, its internal system works to classify and weigh budgets in accordance to the country's methodology. Well-designed IT systems can also help to ensure compliance with new tagging requirements. For example, Bangladesh uses an integrated budgeting and accounting system (IBAS++) climate change module to tag its expenditures (Box 15). In other contexts, systems can help to more easily monitor and share expenditure data. In Ghana, for example, the climate calculator (CLIMATRONIC) allows users to track climate-related expenditures in real time allowing government information to be shared more easily (Government of Ghana, 2018[40]).

Understanding that reforms to internal IT systems may have significant cost dimensions, it is important for countries to identify whether it is feasible to modify current systems when undergoing tagging efforts. Where the internal budget management systems cannot be modified, or do not yet have the functionality to support tagging, countries can still move forward. For example, in France, the government tags all budget items on an Excel spreadsheet.

Box 15. Bangladesh's Integrated Budgeting and Accounting System

Bangladesh tracks all climate finance expenditures through the use of its Integrated Budgeting and Accounting System (IBAS++) in line with the country's Climate Change Strategic Action Plan. Where previously tagging was manually done by the Finance Division, the system has helped to build capacity across the government by allowing dedicated budget officers from line ministries to input relevant project expenditures into the system where it is then automatically weighed and assigned its climate relevance. Information generated by the system is then reviewed by a dedicated unit within the Ministry of Finance to validate and track all expenditures for analysis.

There is also the issue of organising the collection of new data when they are missing (an ecosystem that reaches beyond the governmental organisation per se).

2.7. Building a bridge between green budget tagging and statistical tagging

When designing an approach to green budget tagging, it can be useful to consider its linkages with existing statistical standards. Where tagging aligns with international approaches to categorise spending, for example, this allows opportunities for comparability across countries, facilitating greater transparency and accountability with regard to the actions being taken by a country to achieve green objectives.

Though budget tagging practices are largely country-specific and vary widely across countries, some common international approaches are used to categorise or define budget items and that build on agreed definitions, reporting instructions or even classifications. These include the OECD-DAC Rio markers methodology (OECD, n.d.[41]; 2016[13]), the OECD *Policy Instruments for Environment* (PINE) database and its environmental domain tagging,[4] the European Union's climate action taxonomy (European Commission, 2020[42]), and the CPEIR methodology (UNDP, 2015[37]) as well as the multilateral development banks' co-benefit methodology (World Bank, 2011[43]; AfDB et al., 2015[11]). While these international definitions are not always designed to provide internationally comparable data on expenditures that meet a statistical standard,[5] they may still facilitate cross-country comparisons. For instance, the Rio markers, though not fully comparable from a statistical perspective, build on agreed definitions and reporting instructions allowing for opportunities for broader comparisons. In the case of the PINE database, countries report data on taxes, fees and charges, environmentally motivated subsidies, and other policy instruments according to established internationally harmonised definitions (e.g. the System of National Accounts) which are subsequently classified into a dozen environmental domains (e.g. air pollution, climate change, biodiversity) using agreed definitions (OECD, 2017[44]).[6]

Box 16. Statistical tagging

Statistical tagging refers to the use of commonly agreed upon official statistical frameworks and standards when tagging expenditure flows. This tends to categorise expenditure after it has occurred and plays an important role in enabling cross-country assessments of public expenditure flows.

Statistical tagging practices comply with statistical standards in that there is the provision of a comprehensive set of guidelines for data collection, including: a set of definition(s), associated with clear analytical concepts; a set of statistical units; a classification system, ideally connected with other classification systems; coding processes; and output categories, that should include a structure to organise information and relevant indicators, and which may include an accounting framework, such as the System of National Accounts (European Commission et al., 2008[45]; OECD, 2004[46]).

Currently, there are two functional classification systems relevant for implementing statistical tagging (see Box 16): the Classification of Environmental Activities (CEA) and the Classification of the Functions of Government (COFOG). These are used in international statistical frameworks such as the System of Environmental-Economic Accounting, the Financial Statistical Framework (UN et al., 2014[47]).

Although green budget tagging and statistical tagging can serve different primary purposes, there are synergies to exploit. Building bridges between these two types of activities and ensuring a minimum of coherence (for example in terms of definitions and classifications) can help produce better and more comparable international data on climate and environmental expenditure (such as those collected regularly from countries by the OECD and Eurostat in line with the System of Environmental-Economic Accounting and its environmental activity accounts). It would also help improve national data on environmental expenditure. The OECD is currently working with Eurostat and with countries to improve the coverage of climate and biodiversity-related expenditure in its surveys, including by helping countries identify relevant expenditure items in national data sources. The Inter-American Development Bank is currently exploring a methodology for climate budget tagging that can be linked to official statistical frameworks and classifications. This requires exploiting existing classification systems and conceptualising an accounting framework to organise the information (IADB, forthcoming[3]). Using existing statistical classifications and methods does not prevent tailoring green budgeting to national needs and objectives, yet it can ensure common definitions and groupings and thus facilitate the (re)use of data from green budgeting initiatives in reporting on environmental expenditure. In Italy, for example, programmes are assigned a second-level COFOG category to facilitate data usage and international comparison with a screening process, including classification in accordance to CEPA and CReMA classification standards.

Countries can work closely with national statistical offices or central banks to link their budget tagging efforts to these standards and frameworks. This may include identifying a clear definition (and boundaries) for all national climate change actions (which includes other fiscal tools in addition to expenditure) and aligning it to existing standards and methods for mitigation and adaptation. Illustratively, this can mean using existing classifications (CEA) and methods (such as the Environmental Protection Expenditure Accounts for environmental protection activities) for mitigation activities and developing a list of activities along COFOG and/or ISIC (International Standard Industrial Classification) for national adaptation and risk management actions. To further distinguish between environmental protection mitigation actions and harmful actions, countries can utilise CEA domains as a basis of whether actions positively or negatively affect the environment. Likewise, the OECD PINE database can inform on tagging by "green" domains, and the OECD Inventory of Fossil Fuel Support Measures on fossil fuel-related direct and indirect subsidies.

3. Using the information from green budget tagging

The information produced by green budget tagging can be powerful when it is fed into policy making and budget decisions. Using the information for awareness raising alone is unlikely to achieve substantial results and will not justify the time and effort that is involved. Resch et al. (2017[30]) point out: "Whatever the expenditure tracking methodology, it should be recognised that, unless the information resulting from the tag, analysis or review is used to inform climate change policy, planning or budgeting, or to strengthen accountability around climate change commitments, it will remain an academic exercise of limited operational value".

This section looks at how green budget tagging can be used alongside other tools to build a larger stock of evidence on programmes relevant to national climate and environmental goals, and their impact. It then considers how this information can be used during budget decision making to improve the performance of government policy and, if desired, to qualify for green finance instruments. Finally, it outlines how the information from tagging can be presented to ensure transparency and facilitate oversight.

3.1. Using green budgeting to build a larger stock of evidence

Green budget tagging is one of many tools that can be employed as part of an overall green budgeting framework to help build a larger stock of evidence on how budget measures contribute to or deter from green objectives. A number of tools can work alongside green budget tagging to facilitate better understanding of the effectiveness of different measures and support budgetary decisions that align with policy goals, including: impact assessments, cost-benefit analysis, and a green dimension to performance setting or performance budgeting.

There are different types of impact assessments that can help inform budget decisions, including environmental impact assessments and carbon impact assessments. Environmental impact assessments can serve as a means to highlight the environmental impact of individual policies and programmes. Examples of this include the EU Directive on Strategic Environmental Assessment, which requests the assessment of policy plans or programmes for likely significant effects on the environment and the reasonable alternatives. Carbon impact assessments include methodologies to assess the impact of budget measures on GHG emissions.

Another tool that can gather useful evidence for budget decision making is cost-benefit analysis of projects and policies that have a deliberate aim of environmental improvement or are actions that affect, even indirectly, the natural environment. It helps decision makers to have a clearer picture of how society would fare under a range of policy options for achieving particular goals and improve policy responses. *Ex ante* cost-benefit analysis can be supported by an *ex post* assessment to cast light on the accuracy of the *ex ante* answer, or whatever decision rule was used to justify the policy or project (OECD, 2018[48]).

A green dimension to performance setting, or performance budgeting, can also ensure that there is due consideration to including climate or environmental indicators and objectives as part of the government's performance framework. It also encourages regular data collection in relation to key environmental metrics, providing a basis for performance monitoring, impact evaluation and better budget decision making (OECD, 2019[49]). In this regard, countries can draw from experiences of gender budgeting, where countries such as Austria and Iceland require that each budget chapter have a performance measure related to gender equality.

While these tools may have been in place for a number of years, the evidence they provide can be underutilised. Where green budget tagging is introduced in the context of political momentum for improving how the budget supports green objectives, it can provide additional impetus for incorporating consideration of the evidence it provides in budget decision making.

3.2. Using this evidence to inform budget decision making and improve performance

The evidence gathered from green budget tagging and complimentary green budgeting tools is most valuable when it serves as a direct input to budget allocation decisions or as contextual information to inform budget planning, and to instil greater transparency and accountability throughout the budget process, by providing information to legislators and the public on how the budget contributes to national climate or environmental objectives. For this to work, the evidence, and analysis flowing from it should be available for relevant stakeholders at the time that they take key budget decisions. The evidence gathered through these tools can also provide input into processes designed to improve the performance of government policy, including programme evaluation and public expenditure or spending reviews.

3.2.1. Inputting evidence into different stages of the budget cycle

Information gathered through green budget tagging and other tools that support green budgeting can be input into the different stages of the government's annual budget cycle to support the allocation of public resources in line with strategic priorities.

This information has a potential role at each stage of the budget cycle, as shown in Figure 3. The first stage that the evidence gathered through tools supporting green budgeting can be used for is the budget planning stage. Lessons from the Philippines show how tagging can inform budget planning and allocation decisions (Box 17). Other examples are provided by Pakistan, where the Ministry of Water has used information from climate budget tagging to integrate climate change into its medium-term budgetary framework. In Indonesia, the Ministry of Finance used climate budget tagging data to identify the gap between the existing public spending and the estimated cost of the national climate mitigation action (UNDP, 2019[8]).

> **Box 17. The use of budgeting evidence in budget allocation decisions in the Philippines**
>
> Each year, the Department of Budget and Management, as part of its budget preparation process, requires government agencies to provide an overview of their climate-relevant expenditures (previous, current and succeeding fiscal year). Climate-relevant programmes, activities and projects are then classified according to their allotment type (personnel services, maintenance and other operating expenses, financial expenses, and capital outlays). As part of this process, government agencies are requested to summarise and present their climate-related programme budget requests during technical budget hearings.
>
> Source: World Bank (forthcoming[2]).

The next stage of the budget cycle is the budget approval phase. Here, information from tools such as green budget tagging can be used to instil greater transparency and accountability; for example, through facilitating the provision of a green budget statement accompanying the draft budget proposal (see Section 3.4).

During the implementation stage of the budget, information can be used to inform in-year adjustments. An example of the information from green budget tagging being used in this way is provided by Honduras, where the information generated through the tagging system appears to inform mid-year reallocations between climate change projects (World Bank, forthcoming[2]).

Finally, in the audit stage of the budget, information from green budgeting can be used to inform scrutiny of budget execution, and follow-up decisions on policy design and resource allocation in subsequent years.

Figure 3. Role for evidence from green budgeting at different stages of the budget cycle

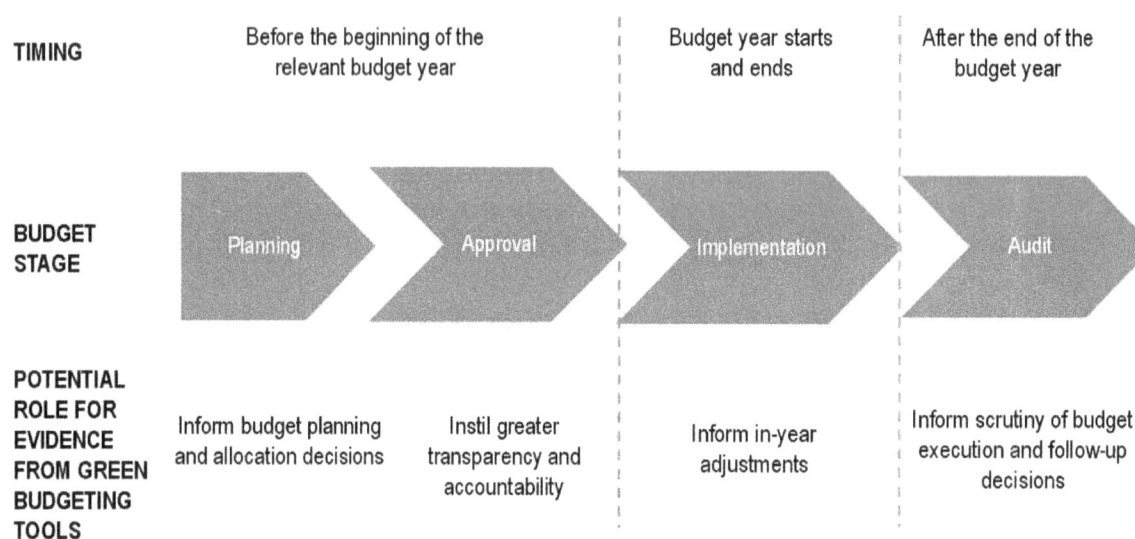

TIMING	Before the beginning of the relevant budget year	Budget year starts and ends	After the end of the budget year
BUDGET STAGE	Planning → Approval	Implementation	Audit
POTENTIAL ROLE FOR EVIDENCE FROM GREEN BUDGETING TOOLS	Inform budget planning and allocation decisions / Instil greater transparency and accountability	Inform in-year adjustments	Inform scrutiny of budget execution and follow-up decisions

3.2.2. Using information to improve the performance of government policy

Green budget tagging does not account for the effectiveness of budget measures. However, information from green budget tagging and other tools supporting green budgeting can also be used in budget processes such as spending or public expenditure reviews, programme evaluations and other analysis to help guide the efficiency and effectiveness in public budgeting. For example, information from green budget tagging can complement output and outcome performance information to give a more detailed picture of the progress towards climate and environmental policy, or as the basis for reviewing programme performance. Or mitigation expenditure by programme can be compared with how much GHG emission reductions are achieved for each programme, giving insights into relative value for money (UNDP, 2019[8]). Information from green budget tagging could also feed into spending reviews, a tool increasingly being used to increase the fiscal space available to government to finance its policy priorities (OECD, 2019[50]). For example, budget tagging might inform a thematic spending review relating to a specific climate or environmental priority of relevant budget measures that should be considered. Alternatively, tagging might help inform a broad spending review on the extent to which an overall package of measures contributes to different strategic objectives.

3.3. Using information to qualify for green finance instruments

A green bond is a type of debt instrument whose proceeds are exclusively earmarked to fund projects that deliver benefits to efforts related to climate change mitigation or adaptation; natural resource depletion; loss of biodiversity; air, water or soil pollution. Some countries have developed the use of green bonds as a key tool to channel investments to green assets in pursuit of their national climate and environmental objectives. In many instances, tagging processes go hand-in-hand with a country's effort on green bonds (see Box 18 for the example of Ireland).

Box 18. Ireland's use of green bonds

In October 2018, the Irish National Treasury Management Agency launched the country's first sovereign green bond, where any proceeds raised can be devoted to eligible "green" expenditure with the government reporting to investors through annual allocation reports. These commitments made it necessary for Ireland to track all government expenditure on climate-related matters on an ongoing basis. In tracking government expenditure, to ensure consistency and alignment to the requirement of managing green bonds, Ireland utilised the International Capital Markets Association standard definition of "green expenditure" as the basis for its budget tagging classification methodology.

Source: Cremins and Kevany (2018[21]).

The information from green budget tagging can help strengthen a country's framework for green bonds by providing a set of considerations for identifying the eligibility of projects, tracking finances and reporting. For example, Indonesia's Ministry of Finance and National Development Planning Agency relied on its existing climate budget tagging system to assess projects eligible to be financed from its Green Sukuk (Indonesia's green bond) as well as ensuring that associated projects are in accordance with the tenor of the Green Sukuk (UNDP, 2019[8]). However, although tagging efforts have been one of many tools used to support countries' green finance initiatives and pursuit of green bonds, these do not necessarily require the use of green budget tagging.

3.4. Ensuring the results of green budgeting are transparent and open to independent oversight

As mentioned in Section 3.2, green budget tagging can help instil greater transparency and accountability during the budget process where the information or analysis from the exercise is made public. The provision of this in the form of a green budget statement (GBS) or a citizens' climate or environmental budget can ensure that analysis is presented in a user-friendly way and is open to scrutiny by external stakeholders such as parliament and citizens.

3.4.1. Green budget statements

A GBS can be used to show summary information from green budget tagging. In this way, stakeholders can assess how the draft budget contributes to national climate or environmental objectives. Where the information and analysis drawn from green budget tagging is presented in a GBS or citizens' budget, this can support greater transparency, accountability and public engagement on budget policy.

These statements may be published as part of the draft budget proposal, serving as one element contributing to deliberations at the approval phase of the budget cycle. Examples of countries that have already introduced a GBS in the form of chapters or supplementary reports to accompany the draft budget to provide an overview of relevant budget measures and their impact on climate and the environment are provided in Box 19.

Box 19. Examples of green budget statements

France: In order to enhance its reporting on the overall impact of public finance measures on the ecological transition, the French government developed a more comprehensive and updated yearly "Green Budget" for the 2021 Budget. The document mainly draws on the information gathered from green budget tagging, and also provides additional information such as the economic effect of environmental taxes on households and firms.

Bangladesh: In Bangladesh, the publication of an annual *Climate Financing for Sustainable Development* report generated from green budget tagging has helped to engage civil society to hold government accountable. The report presents the percentage of climate-related spending subsumed in total public expenditure, with the purpose of showing the government's commitment to address the adverse effects of climate change. The report also intends to add to the knowledge and understanding of climate finance among a wider range of stakeholders in Bangladesh so they can be better engaged with and contribute to policy development and monitoring and hold decision makers to account.

Nicaragua: Final expenditures of activities linked to climate change and disaster risk reduction and environmental management are compiled and reflected in the government's general liquidation report submitted to the National Assembly. This becomes subject to future audits by the General Comptroller.

Philippines: A climate budget brief, detailing climate change allocations, funding gaps and recommendations in relation to the National Climate Change Plan, is used to inform budget hearings. This coincides with a proposed climate budget as part of the President's Budget to Congress as part of the annual budget process.

Sources: Government of France (2019[51]); Ministry of Finance of Bangladesh (2020[52]); World Bank (forthcoming[2]).

In addition to information and analysis from green budget tagging, a GBS could include information such as:

- **A general green budget statement:** summarises in broad narrative terms how measures introduced in the budget are intended to support green priorities and goals.
- **A green progress statement:** provides a more detailed exposition of how the budget measures advance the government's green agenda, by reference to established objectives and indicators.
- **Distributional impact analysis:** offers an assessment of how specific green measures (both revenue and expenditure) affect individuals, households or firms.

3.4.2. Citizens' budgets

Citizens' budgets have been introduced to present to the budget in a way that makes sense to the general public and improve government accountability. Some countries, such as Bangladesh and Nepal, have now also introduced a "Citizens' Climate Budget" to help bring about awareness of government action towards climate objectives. Lessons from Bangladesh highlight how green budget tagging can serve as a useful tool to engage and inform the public in this regard (Box 20).

Box 20. Bangladesh's Citizens' Climate Budget

The Ministry of Finance, in conjunction with the *Climate Financing for Sustainable Development* report, published a "Citizens' Climate Budget" for the 2018/19 and 2019/20 budgets. It provided a concise summary of climate-related budget allocations for the current and upcoming fiscal year, as well as information on actual expenditures of previous budget cycles. The tagging has raised awareness of the government's commitment to climate action – creating a demand for more information and more impact assessments from civil society organisations. In fact, it was only after demands by civil society to include more accurate expenditure figures did the government include actual expenditure information as part of its reports to the public.

Sources: World Bank (forthcoming[2]); UNDP (2019[8]).

4. Key challenges in designing and implementing green budget tagging

In designing and implementing an approach to green budget tagging, some aspects pose greater challenges and it is important to be aware of these, and prepare for them. This section identifies the most prominent challenge, and how they can be addressed. In particular, it looks at the challenges of identifying the appropriate level of granularity for tagging, deciding what to do with budget measures relating to adaptation; tagging negative budget measures; and balancing environmental, social and economic objectives.

4.1. Identifying the appropriate level of granularity for tagging

One of the key challenges faced by countries in implementing green budget tagging is identifying the appropriate level of granularity for budget measures to be tagged. Tagging broader budget lines on the one hand provides a high-level overview of budget alignment to green goals, but sacrifices granularity and overlooks the fact that different activities within the budget line may have different or even contrary effects on environmental and climate goals. For instance, should a country tag a budget line as contributing to climate or environmental objectives where only a portion of activities are relevant, external stakeholders may accuse the government of "greenwashing" expenditures. Should it not tag the budget line, then the government may have concerns that the tagging process does not include the full set of programmes which address the country's climate objectives. Decisions on tagging can also be challenging when budget items are difficult to classify or where additional funding is provided in a budget line to make it climate sensitive (UNDP, 2019[8]). France, for example, noted the challenges of identifying whether budget lines relating to housing projects positively or negatively impact its green objectives.

Tagging at a more granular level is often more attractive, given that it provides greater levels of accuracy. However, it also brings its own risks, given that it requires greater resources (in terms of time and capacity for tagging). Additionally, considerations for the breadth (the number of sectors to be counted) creates an added dimension for countries along with the depth (level of granularity) of coverage.

Given the challenges of both broad and granular tagging, countries have to select an approach which balances their need for accuracy with the need to operate within the government's capacity, as well as the purpose of the tagging (e.g. mainstreaming, accountability and transparency). Decisions on the appropriate level of granularity can be taken in tandem with decisions on the appropriate weighting system in order to reduce trade-offs. For example, when tagging at a higher level, using a weighting system which allows only part of the budget item to be included facilitates greater understanding of the budget's alignment towards green objectives.

4.2. Deciding how to deal with budget measures relating to disaster risk management and adaptation

When designing a tagging approach, it is important to consider the extent to which spending related to disaster risk management and adaptation efforts are consistent and coherent with a country's national environmental and climate goals and therefore how they should be tagged. One of the reasons that this activity is difficult to categorise is because it is contextual and differs for each country, depending on its needs. This can be particularly challenging as potentially many government actions can count towards adaptation efforts (e.g. health and education programmes along with flood prevention measures). In addition, one country's efforts may also have negative externalities for another country – raising the importance to consider spillover effects of adaptation measures.[7] For example, building a floodwall in a region may be appropriate to prevent instances of future flooding, but can have negative spillovers to the local ecosystem and biodiversity and affect neighbouring regions' ability to adapt to climate change. In other cases, certain measures considered effective today may have negative consequences in the future or likewise, measures considered effective by a majority of society may undermine the resilience of ethnic minority groups. As such, it may be important to consider the risks of maladaptation, where adaptation actions can serve to potentially exacerbate existing vulnerabilities to climate change.

Furthermore, tagging certain mitigation or adaption measures may largely depend on the country's specific methodology, as many of these dimensions (particularly in the development context) can be counted towards development interventions (e.g. expanding electricity via renewable energy or ecosystem rehabilitation to reduce flooding) (World Bank, forthcoming[2]). Thus, there is a strong argument for tagging disaster risk management and adaptation measures separately from mitigation activities.

4.3. Tagging negative budget measures

Most countries do not tag budget measures which make a negative contribution to climate and environmental goals. Given that the intent and purpose of green budget tagging is often to help inform decisions, not having a sense of areas which negatively contribute to a country's green objectives limits the ability to have a full understanding of a country's progress. For example, analysis in Finland and Indonesia has shown that negative expenditures can outweigh positive climate expenditures (World Bank, forthcoming[2]). Oftentimes, this includes overlooking budget measures related to fossil fuel subsidies, as well as agricultural and construction measures. For example, Finland has recently found that its budget contains about EUR 3.5 billion of harmful energy subsidies, twice the amount dedicated to subsidies for becoming carbon-neutral and resource-wise (Finnish Ministry of Finance, 2019[53]; Annukka et al., 2019[54]). In Ireland, a study analysed several scenarios on increases in carbon taxes and removal of fossil fuel subsidies. Results showed that removing fossil fuel subsidies would lower total economy-wide CO_2 emissions by 20% in 2030. Emissions were estimated to be 31% lower in 2030 if an increase in the carbon tax was added to the removal of the fossil fuel subsidies (de Bruin, Monaghan and Yakut, 2019[55]).

To overcome this challenge, it is recommended, as a starting point, to identify priority sectors and large expenditure areas which are known to already have a negative impact on climate change, such as fossil fuel subsidies and programmes which facilitate deforestation, mining and burning coal (UNDP, 2019[8]). The OECD, the International Monetary Fund and the World Bank continue to work with countries to assist in this effort. The OECD identifies over 1 300 budgetary transfers, tax breaks and spending programmes providing support to the production and consumption of coal, oil, gas and other petroleum products in 44 OECD and G20 economies to shed light on how public resources are used (OECD, 2020[56]; 2020[57]). Government support for the production and consumption of fossil fuels in these 44 advanced and emerging economies remains high, at USD 178 billion based on 2019 figures, representing a 10% increase from 2018. This increase was dominated by a 38% year-on-year rise of direct and indirect support for fossil fuel production, predominantly in OECD countries (OECD, 2020[57]). The International Monetary Fund, which incorporates external cost estimations such as road use and congestion costs and health impacts of air pollution in its estimates of fossil fuel support, found in its assessment that global subsidies remained high, at USD 4.7 trillion in 2017, with three-quarters of subsidies due to domestic factors such as energy pricing reform (Coady et al., 2019[58]). In other contexts, countries have relied on the World Bank's Energy Subsidy Reform Assessment Framework to identify and quantify energy subsidies in relation to their impact and to evaluate the enabling environment for reform efforts (ESMAP, n.d.[59]). Though these initial approaches may rely on subjective judgements of programmes, just as in categorising positive expenditure, it provides an opportunity to balance the discussion among decision makers. An example of a country that is tagging negative budget measures is France (Box 21).

Box 21. Tagging negative expenditures in France

In 2017, France committed to the Paris Collaborative on Green Budgeting, launched by the OECD, to assess the compatibility of its public finance trajectories with the Paris Agreement and other environmental goals. As part of these efforts, France experimented a methodology in 2019 and then developed its first comprehensive "green budget" as part of the 2021 Budget that provides an overview of budget measures and their alignment with France's green objectives. Specifically, measures are categorised according to the extent to which they have a favourable or negative impact on six environmental dimensions. The scale is shown below:

> **3: Very favourable**, environmentally targeted expenses

> **2: Favourable**, no explicit environmental target, but indirect positive impact

> **1: Favourable but controversial**, e.g. short-term favourable effects but presence of a long-term technology lock in risk

> **0: Neutral**, no significant impact of information

> **-1: Unfavourable**, environmentally harmful expenditure

Sources: Ministry of Ecological Transition (2020[20]); Government of France (2020[60]).

4.4. Ensuring consistency and quality of tagging

Budget tagging processes are often subjective and susceptible to significant exclusion and inclusion errors. Furthermore, localised approaches and different methodologies make it difficult to compare across countries and in some cases, within countries across sectors. In some situations, the subjective nature of tagging can give opportunity for "greenwashing" or result in undertagging. For instance, tagging programmes on coal mine dismantling as having a positive impact towards green objectives may be viewed with scepticism by certain stakeholders.

Clear guidance for green budget tagging, together with support on how to deal with the more ambiguous budget lines, and validation processes can help (as outlined in Section 2.3). While this can increase capacity requirements (World Bank, forthcoming[2]), these actions help build the system's credibility. For example, reviews by senior officials may provide incentives to improve the quality of the tagging as well as increase the visibility of the process to facilitate appropriate engagement across all levels of government.

As part of the continuous improvement process, it can be useful to conduct internal *ex post* checks that help improve tagging processes over time. External stakeholders may also be able to help, such as the supreme audit institution, parliament, independent fiscal institution or civil society. These stakeholders may do so through general scrutiny of tagging reports or by conducting *ex post* reviews, audits and evaluations that provide a view on the correctness of tagging. A good practice example is provided by Bangladesh, where performance audits have been introduced for certain climate-tagged projects with a pilot currently also being discussed in Pakistan (World Bank, forthcoming[2]).

4.5. Balancing environmental, social and economic objectives

It is important to remember that the information from green budget tagging highlights how budget measures contribute to environmental objectives, but these measures have varying impacts on broader social and economic objectives. It may be that budget measures contributing to environmental objectives also have positive social and economic benefits. In particular, there are often benefits for future generations, who would otherwise be affected through the damaging effects of climate change (IMF, 2013[61]). Recent events have illustrated that there can also at times be tensions between these objectives. For example, France's efforts to adopt carbon taxes have been met with social opposition from the *Gilets Jaunes* protests as a result of the increased tax burden they placed on the working class with limited access to public transportation, in context to concurrent a rise in fuel prices. In other instances, pursuits for climate or environmental goals conflict with policies aimed at addressing inequality. In efforts to address some of these tensions, Ireland has an approach to use revenues from carbon taxes to protect communities most at risk – bringing wider social acceptance to carbon tax increases.

Green budget tagging can be useful in identifying budget measures which negatively impact green goals (e.g. fuel subsidies), stimulating reforms in this area. To ensure that work such as green budget tagging does not inadvertently give rise to social or economic tensions, the evidence that it provides should not be considered alone in decision making. Instead, the information should be used to frame policy discussions on how to reduce the negative environmental impact while managing any associated social and economic trade-offs. These can be in the form of identifying plans to phase out subsidies over time, as observed in Ecuador (Box 22). Consideration should be given to the socio-economic implications of different options.

Box 22. Understanding the distributional impact of subsidy reform in Ecuador

With 7% of Ecuador's annual spending comprised of energy subsidies, identifying ways to reduce the amount of public spending on subsidies can yield economic and environmental benefits. However, given perceptions that subsidy reductions are felt by the most vulnerable households, reforms have been met with political resistance. A study by the Inter-American Development Bank found that energy subsidies, in absolute terms, largely benefit richer households. By shifting funding from subsidies to an existing social protection programme (Bono de Desarrollo Humano) by about USD 50 per month, a net benefit of almost 10% is felt by those in the poorest quintile. The study recommended reforms to eliminate subsidies on gasoline while increasing transfers to vulnerable households and replacing liquefied petroleum gas (LPG) subsidies with targeted LPG vouchers that can benefit the poorest 40% of households in the country.

Source: Schaffitzel et al. (2019[62]).

---

5. Elements that can support an effective approach to green budget tagging

Lessons from efforts to undertake public financial management (PFM) reforms in the past, and in particular from countries introducing green budget tagging, have provided insights into elements that can support an effective approach. This section highlights some of those key elements, including: strong political and administrative leadership, a scaled approach to implementation, ensuring coherence with wider PFM reforms and complementing tagging with a wider set of government reforms to achieve national goals.

5.1. Strong political and administrative leadership

Political buy-in can support the viability and credibility of any new reform and green budget tagging is no exception. Stand-alone tagging exercises that are not part of the broader political economy of the country risk being efforts that are not fully utilised and implemented – instead being considered "tick the box" exercises.

Ensuring political leadership in relation to green objectives, and processes such as green budget tagging which support their achievement, provides weight to their importance and helps administrative implementation of the tagging across the government (UNDP, 2019[8]). An example is provided by France, where the president has helped initiate the introduction of green budget tagging following his strong political commitment at the One Planet Summit in 2017.

While political leadership is important, particularly at the beginning, administrative leadership by the central budget authority and the Ministry of the Environment or Climate Change helps embed the initiative over time. This is illustrated from experiences of implementing gender budgeting (Box 23).

Lessons from gender budgeting show that legal foundations can also ensure sustainability in the longer term. For example, legislation that is fully tested and debated in parliament has helped embed gender budgeting as a valued and enduring feature of public policy making and insulate it, as far as possible, from fluctuations arising from the economic or political environment (Downes and Nicol, 2019[63]). This can be observed in the case of the Philippines, where the Climate Change Act of 2012 required the Department of Budget and Management to "undertake the formulation of the national budget in a way that ensures the appropriate prioritisation and allocation of funds to support climate change-related programs and projects in the annual program of government". This has helped the Philippines to set the basis for a broader climate budgeting approach.

Box 23. Strong leadership and its role in supporting gender budgeting in Canada

Canada introduced gender budgeting in 2016. A central tool of Canada's approach to gender budgeting are *ex ante* gender impact assessments of policies (GBA+).

The Department of Finance has showed strong leadership from the start in relation to these reforms. At the beginning, to ensure that the line ministries were clear on new requirements, the Minister of Finance stipulated in the budget circular that all new budget proposals must be accompanied by a GBA+.

The Department of Finance then set about trying to improve the quality of the information that it was receiving as part of the gender budgeting reforms. For example, in Budget 2018, the Department of Finance highlighted that there was inconsistency in the quality and application of GBA+ analysis accompanying budget proposals. Furthermore, the department highlighted examples of GBA+ analysis where there was room for improvement and made a commitment to publish GBA+ accompanying all budget proposals starting in Budget 2019. This public "naming and shaming" and commitment to transparency on the information accompanying budget proposals helped ensure that spending departments took the new requirements seriously and gender budgeting is now becoming an exercise which brings high-quality information to inform budget decisions supporting Canada's gender goals.

Sources: Government of Canada (2019[64]); OECD (2018[65]).

5.2. A scaled approach to implementation

Another element which can support effective implementation of green budgeting is a scaled approach to implementation, whereby countries start small and iterate and expand their efforts over time (as outlined in Section 2.4). Mindful that bureaucratic resistance and limited capacity are some of the main challenges when initiating reforms, this allows countries to develop capacity over time, and tailor the approach. In general, it is observed that this is how countries are implementing green budget tagging. For instance, in Ireland, the government started by tagging expenditures with a positive impact on climate change, but is moving to tag negative expenditures over time as it develops sufficient capacity and expertise. In the Philippines, the government recognised from the start that reforms are likely to be accomplished over the medium to long term. As such, the Department for Budget and Management and Climate Change Commission focused on generating concrete products quickly to engage stakeholders across the budget process. Like Ireland, due to the novel nature of the tagging process, the initial approach was limited to only positive expenditures, with plans to add in tax expenditures and negative expenditures in subsequent years. A further example is given by Nepal's implementation of climate budget tagging (Box 24).

Box 24. Nepal's scaled approach to implementing climate budget tagging

Nepal started implementing climate budget tagging along a simplified approach using 11 criteria to define and share climate-relevant activities, serving as the basis to define the weight of each programme. Building on this, the Ministry of Agriculture is piloting an expansion of the existing criteria based on seven agriculture-specific typologies, with relevance being determined along three non-financial factors:

1. the degree to which an activity targets the correct beneficiaries
2. whether it links to a climate change policy
3. whether it is based on a climate risk assessment.

As the pilot with the Ministry of Agriculture develops, Nepal plans to evolve its original methodology to other ministries so that tagging processes are attuned to different sectors.

Source: UNDP (2019[8]).

5.3. Ensuring coherence with wider public financial mangement reforms

Many PFM systems have undergone significant reforms in recent decades, particularly since the 2008 global financial crisis. Reforms have focused on introducing elements such as programme budgeting, performance budgeting, medium-term planning, increased transparency, and greater parliamentary and public participation in the budget process (OECD, 2019[66]).

Some PFM systems support green budget tagging more easily than others. For example, countries with existing programme budgeting are better able to incorporate green budget tagging processes than traditional input-based systems. This is echoed in experiences with gender and SDG budgeting, where existing programme-based structures have helped to adopt implementation of additional high-level areas of focus (Stotsky, 2016[67]). It can also be easier in countries where there are stronger links between planning and budgeting. In sequencing PFM reforms, it is thus helpful to introduce tagging after developments to implement programme budgeting and to link planning with budgeting. Lessons from the implementation of gender budgeting in low-capacity settings also show that there are often greater challenges where a country has weak public expenditure management systems and political economy factors in budget management (vested interests) (World Bank, forthcoming[2]).

Initiatives to implement green budgeting and green budget tagging are also part of a wider momentum that has gathered for a set of budgeting approaches focused on specific priorities, sometimes termed "budgeting for high-level priorities". Examples include gender budgeting, SDG budgeting and well-being budgeting. These approaches look to embed more systematic linkages between budget decision making and high-level cross-cutting priorities – including through developing greater awareness and capacity to consider these priorities across government, building greater evidence and using this to take more informed decision making during the budget process.

In general, tagging exercises can support the implementation of other PFM reforms, such as performance budgeting, or developing a medium-term expenditure framework, since it provides information on financial resources allocated to high-level policy priorities. This facilitates linking spending and policy objectives as well as measuring results from budget policy (UNDP, 2015[37]). Where information is presented to the public, for example through a statement accompanying the budget or as part of a citizens' budget, it can also support PFM reforms to improve budget transparency and increase accountability and public engagement on how the government is using budget policy to ensure that national climate and environmental goals are prioritised and achieved.

When green budgeting is being implemented and there are already other budget tagging approaches in place, it can be helpful to develop a coherent approach. An example of a coherent approach for tagging multiple dimensions is provided by Iceland, where expenditure is tagged for links to both the SDGs and gender equality. To facilitate a coherent approach, Iceland has developed an IT system which line ministries can use to tag expenditure as relevant to these higher level priorities.

In other instances, countries may be able to use green budget tagging as a model for expanding tagging to other priorities. In Ecuador, for example, there is consideration to scale climate budget tagging to other areas of the SDGs. This is a natural evolution given that the cross-cutting goals of climate and the environment are linked to a number of SDGs. There is also often intersectionality between climate and environmental goals and other high-level priorities, with women, those in poverty, people with disabilities and ethnic minorities often disproportionately affected by climate change and environmental degradation. This builds the case for approaches to green budget tagging that allow measures to be tagged for other dimensions such as gender, poverty or the SDGs (UNDP, 2019[8]). In this way, green budget tagging can provide for a better understanding and discussion around how different policy interventions on climate and the environment impact different socio-economic groups, as recommended in Section 4.5.

5.4. Complementing green budget tagging with a wider set of government reforms to achieve national goals

Government spending, together with fiscal instruments including taxes, charges, pricing externalities and subsidies, all have the potential to influence progress towards green objectives. To the extent that there is information related to these fiscal policy choices in the budget, green budget tagging can shine an important spotlight on how fiscal policy as a whole is impacting green objectives. However, where transparency on these items falls short, the effectiveness of green budget tagging is affected.

A key area where information is often limited is tax expenditures. Although these can have wide-ranging implications for green objectives, for example tax benefits for fossil fuels, the quality and scope of reporting varies considerably among countries. To ensure that tools such as green budgeting help highlight the alignment between fiscal policy and green objectives, governments must significantly improve their reporting on tax expenditures.

However, the budget is not the only public policy intervention to support progress towards climate and environmental goals. In addition to ensuring that green budget tagging captures the full range of fiscal instruments impacting green objectives, tools such as green budgeting and green budget tagging can be complimented with wider efforts outside the budget process to be most effective. Other interventions might include the use of infrastructure and public procurement policies, as well as assessing, amending or introducing regulations, market-based policy instruments or legislation so that they better support the achievement of national climate and environmental goals.

Infrastructure and public procurement policies can help leverage existing efforts toward green objectives. Infrastructure investments, for example, can mobilise private resources in areas such of sustainable transport and energy. In other contexts, setting specific green conditionality measures to infrastructure programmes can ensure that various dimensions of environmental and climate change objectives are incorporated throughout project cycles. For example, the Netherlands and the United States have incorporated biodiversity points and estimates for cost-benefit analysis to infrastructure projects (Frits and Ruijs, 2019[68]; OECD, 2019[69]). Public procurements, accounting for a sizeable portion of public expenditures, can also be aligned to address green objectives. Sustainability criteria within procurement processes, for instance, can ensure that supply chains meet and address standards for reducing waste and emissions and protect biodiversity (OECD, 2015[70]). Regulation can be put in place to control emissions, and constrain or ban polluting activities and chemicals that are toxic for people and the environment. Regulatory scans or reviews can help identify actions that are needed to ensure that regulations are coherent with, and support the achievement of, green goals. Direct regulation can also be supported by innovative market-based policy instruments to meet public policy objectives. Well-designed, market-based instruments such as tradable permits, and deposit-refund systems have proven to be at least as environmentally effective as direct regulation, and often much more economically efficient (i.e. meeting given environmental objectives at lower cost).

Reviewing, amending and developing new legislation also helps to ensure that the legal system reflects the changing environmental context and supports the achievement of green objectives. For example, Denmark recently passed new and ambitious climate legislation that enshrined a commitment to reduce carbon emissions by 70% by 2030 in law and will act as the new framework for Danish climate policy in the years to come (Danish Ministry of Climate, Energy and Utilities, 2020[71]).

Even where strong regulations and legislation are in place, governments are prone to taking policy and decisions that are not coherent with green objectives, e.g. through continuing to support investment in fossil fuels or road building. Some countries are taking efforts to avoid this. For example, New Zealand stated in 2019 that all its major Cabinet decisions will now be taken through a climate change lens. Decision making will be supported by climate impact assessments that are now mandatory for policy and legislative proposals designed to reduce carbon emissions, or which are likely to have an impact on emissions greater than 250 000 tonnes a year (New Zealand Government, 2019[72]).

Where a whole-of-government approach is built, encompassing legal, regulatory, policy and budget decisions, it has significantly more potential to be effective than the implementation of one stand-alone tool.

6. Bringing it all together: Ten principles underpinning an effective approach to green budget tagging

Many countries are still at the early stages of green budget tagging. This report has set out detailed guidance for countries on how to take budget tagging forward most effectively, drawing together the lessons from the international budgeting community, and benefiting from insights from other PFM reforms. The following principles synthesise this guidance. They provide a reference tool for those designing, implementing and improving green budget tagging systems that can meet the challenges of the future. The overall intention is to provide a useful reference tool for policy makers and practitioners around the world, seeking to develop green budget tagging systems that help track how budget measures impact on national climate and environmental objectives. This can help to ensure that public resources are planned, managed and used effectively to make a positive impact on national goals.

The ten principles underpinning an effective approach to green budget tagging

1. To foster national ownership, the decision to start green budget tagging should be driven by national priorities. Countries can benefit from the study of existing models, experiences and international standards, using these to guide an approach that fits their own national context.

2. In designing the tagging system, categories should align with country-specific climate or environmental goals (such as those relating to biodiversity, water and air quality). This allows evidence to be collected on how budget measures contribute to national goals.

3. A weighting system can help address the reality that some budget measures only partially contribute towards climate or environmental goals.

4. Countries should work towards tagging both positive and negative budget measures across the whole budget, or at least priority sectors, such as agriculture, transport, energy and the environment if capacity is insufficient. Where possible, disaster risk management and adaptation measures should be tagged separately from mitigation measures.

5. Green budget tagging efforts benefit from political commitment, strong leadership and clarity of the roles and responsibilities of different actors across government so that a whole-of-government approach is in place. Training and capacity development are crucial in supporting the public administration in incorporating the tagging exercise into the annual budget process and ensuring that the practice is sustainable.

6. Tagging is subjective by nature, and to ensure consistency, there needs to be clear guidance as well as processes for review and validation. This helps to ensure the robustness of data and allays concerns about "greenwashing".

7. Green budget tagging is one of a number of tools that support green budgeting (such as impact assessments, cost-benefit analysis and green performance indicators) through gathering evidence to facilitate more informed decision making. However, using the evidence for awareness raising alone is unlikely to achieve substantial results, and the focus should be on ensuring the use of this evidence in decision making across key stages in the budget cycle (planning, approval, implementation and audit), and to improve the performance of budget interventions.

8. Green budget tagging is supported by a modern budgetary governance framework, which includes programme budgeting and strong links between planning and budgeting. Any approach should be consistent with the broader budgetary framework and coherent with other PFM initiatives, such as gender budgeting and SDG budgeting.

9. Where the information and analysis drawn from green budget tagging is presented in a green budget statement or citizens' budget, this can support greater transparency, accountability and public engagement on how the government is using budget policy to ensure that national climate and environmental goals are prioritised and achieved.

10. The budget is not the only public policy intervention to support progress towards climate and environmental goals. Tools such as regulations and laws are also important and so green budget tagging should not sit alone, but alongside a wider set of reforms to achieve national goals.

Annex A provides country case studies which illustrate green budget tagging practices in greater depth, and shows practices in respect of these ten principles.

Annex A. Country snapshots

This annex provides a snapshot of green budget tagging practices in select countries, framed around the ten principles outlined in this report. Specifically, it highlights experiences from four countries (in alphabetical order):

- France
- Ireland
- Nepal
- the Philippines.

The diversity of objectives, methods and approaches highlight how country approaches are rooted in national contexts. The experiences of these countries indicate that there is no "silver bullet" to developing a green budget tagging approach – each serves to demonstrate that green budget tagging is still a relatively new practice, with countries continuing to develop their approaches over time. Recent reviews of climate change expenditure tagging have shown that challenges still remain (World Bank, forthcoming[2]). Therefore, it is important to see these snapshots as "guiding posts" (and not an end goal) for designing and implementing an approach to green budget tagging.

France

In light of France's commitment to the global Paris Climate Agreement, France is further prioritising its efforts to address climate change. As a founding member of the OECD Paris Collaborative on Green Budgeting, greater consideration has been given to how to ensure that environmental impacts are taken into account throughout the budget process. In 2018, the French National Assembly and the Senate decided that the French government needed to enhance its reporting on the overall impact of public finance measures on the ecological transition. Since then, France, for the first time, developed a more comprehensive and updated version, known as the "Green Budget", to provide an overview of relevant policies and highlight their alignment with France's green objectives. This looks across policy strategies and budget information covering both public and private spending (investments and current spending) as well a strategy for the country's plans for ecological transition. Following an initial set of pilots with a small subset of ministries and an initial methodological report in 2019 (which did not include harmful budget measures), the government published its full report as part of the 2021 Budget in October 2020. The "Green Budget" includes information on fiscal policy alignment with environmental targets; environmental tax revenue; environmental tax expenditure; and the economic effect of environmental taxes on households and firms.

France has worked on a comprehensive classifications system for environmentally friendly, neutral and potentially harmful budget measures. The approach looks at six different environmental aspects: climate change adaptation, mitigation, biodiversity, the circular economy, water and air quality. It also assesses the potentially negative or positive spill-over effects from one environmental sphere to another. This methodology has been applied for the first time for the budget law 2021 (*projet de loi de finances*) and a new updated "Green Budget" was delivered in late September 2020 preceding parliamentary debate on the 2021 finance bill.

Institutional arrangements have been developed to ensure adequate oversight and engagement. Most notably, the country established the High Council for the Climate (Haut Conseil pour le Climat) to provide independent expertise to the government on climate-related public policies.

Table 2. France's green budget tagging "at a glance"

1.	Driven by national priorities	France's commitment to the Paris Climate Agreement and ecological transition.
2.	Aligned to country-specific green goals	The green budget tagging approach identifies budget measures along six green objectives (in line with the EU taxonomy regulation): climate change adaptation, climate change mitigation, biodiversity, the circular economy, water resource management and pollution.
3.	Weighting system	Binary weighting. Tagged budget measures that impact the climate and environment are counted in full.
4.	Work towards tagging both positive and negative budget measures	Tag expenditures that have a positive, neutral and negative impact on the environment and climate. Categorisation ranges from favourable (direct), favourable (indirect), favourable (but controversial) and neutral to unfavourable.
5.	Political commitment, leadership and clear roles/responsibilities	France is a founding member of the OECD's Paris Collaborative on Green Budgeting. Addressing the environment and climate is one of key priorities of the French government. The Ministry for the Economy and Finance and the Ministry for the Ecological Transition provide joint leadership on green budgeting and the tagging process.
6.	Guidance and process for review and validation	Tagging is conducted by a cross-governmental working group including the Ministry for the Ecological Transition's General Commission for Sustainable Development, the Budget Department, the Tax Legislation Department and the Treasury Department, with validation conducted by line ministries.
7.	Tagging coincides with other tools that support green budgeting	
8.	Supported by modern budgetary governance framework	France has a performance budgeting system where both summary and detailed information on performance objectives, indicators and results for each government programme are published each year for accountability purposes. A medium-term expenditure framework reflects targets for total spending at each level of general government within three- or five-year periods.
9.	Presented in green budget statement or citizens' budget	The "Green Budget", containing information on environmental measures in alignment with environmental targets and budgetary policy, is presented each year to feed the parliamentary debate on the budget.
10.	Budget coincides with other public policy interventions	The state reviews tax measures that are harmful to biodiversity and will propose new tools to allow a gradual transition to a tax regime that will better suit new environmental challenges (the Planning Act of the Environment Round Table and National Biodiversity Plan).

Ireland

One of Ireland's central priorities is to lower greenhouse gas emissions and promote climate-resilient development, in line with the Paris Agreement within the United Nations Framework Convention on Climate Change. In line with this commitment, the Minister for Public Expenditure and Reform and the Minister for Finance committed to implement green budgeting as part of the budgetary and estimates process. Building on existing processes for budgeting for other high-level priorities (e.g. equality budgeting), the Department of Public Expenditure and Reform committed to tracking climate-related expenditure for the 2019 Revised Estimates for Public Services. Driven in part by its purpose on facilitating the country's commitment and use of green bonds, the government adopted ICMA (International Capital Markets Association) standards for classifying climate-related expenditures. As such, the scope of tagging only covers programmes (at the multi-million euro level) which significantly support emissions reductions. This conservative classification approach helps withstand accusations of "greenwashing" by stakeholders. Tagged expenditures are analysed and presented as a table under the Revised Estimates for Public Services, presented to parliament. This helps to promote greater transparency and to serve as an input for decision makers on how to keep Ireland on track towards its climate and environmental commitments. The country aims to iterate its approach with plans to develop a tagging system for negative impact and tax expenditures in subsequent budget years.

Table 3. Ireland's green budget tagging "at a glance"

1.	Driven by national priorities	Ireland's commitment to reduce greenhouse gas emissions and promote climate-resilient development (Paris Agreement). Additionally, the National Treasury Management Agency launched the country's first Irish sovereign green bond where proceeds raised can only be devoted to "green" expenditure which is then reported to investors.
2.	Aligned to country-specific green goals	The Irish government has committed to an average 7% per annum reduction in overall greenhouse gas emissions from 2021 to 2030 (a 51% reduction over the decade), to achieving net-zero emissions by 2050, and to enshrine these commitments in law. The National Mitigation Plan called on the Department of Public Expenditure and Reform (DPER) to monitor and report climate-related expenditure through the exchequer. In addition, a tagging system needed to be in place to facilitate reporting for investors in sovereign green bonds.
3.	Weighting system	Binary weighting. Adopted a conservative classification approach where only those programmes where it is evident that all, or at least the majority, of investment in question supports Ireland's transition to a low-carbon, climate-resilient and environmentally sustainable economy are tagged.
4.	Work towards tagging both positive and negative budget measures	Captures only positive expenditure. Plans are under development to introduce reporting on negative expenditure in future budget years.
5.	Political commitment, leadership and clear roles/responsibilities	Ireland became a member of the OECD's Paris Collaborative on Green Budgeting in 2018. Climate change and the environment remain key political priorities for the government, with several references in the Programme for Government published in June 2020. The DPER plays a key leadership role in relation to green budgeting and the tagging process.
6.	Guidance and process for review and validation	A team of experts within the DPER conducts the initial tagging process, in close co-ordination with the Department of Environment, Climate and Communications. Validation is conducted bilaterally between the DPER and line ministries.
7.	Tagging coincides with other tools that support green budgeting	A national biodiversity expenditure review is underway to estimate expenditures on biodiversity. This will help assess progress towards government commitments on biodiversity and track spending across sectors and departments, non-governmental organisations, and the private sector.
8.	Supported by modern budgetary governance framework	Ireland presents budget information by programme, and already has a system of performance budgeting in place. The budget document (REV) includes output targets alongside financial allocations. An annual performance report shows performance information for each ministry, although these are not yet linked to an overarching performance framework. A medium-term expenditure framework includes three-year rolling ceilings, consistent with fiscal rules.
9.	Presented in green budget statement or citizens' budget	Information from tagging is presented in a table within the Revised Estimates for Public Services, presented annually to the parliament.
10.	Budget coincides with other public policy interventions	The DPER has also worked with government departments receiving funding from carbon tax revenues to develop *ex ante* performance metrics for programmes that have received added funding from carbon tax increases. Plans are in place to undertake *ex post* assessment of performance against selected metrics.

Nepal

Extreme weather events such as floods, droughts and changing rainfall patterns have left Nepal's agricultural system vulnerable to the effects of climate change. Due to limited resources to address many of these challenges, the country underwent efforts to introduce climate budget tagging with a view to this helping it access international climate funds. It was hoped that this could help the Nepali government to finance climate change activities as well as to identify funding gaps for decision makers and stakeholders. Starting from 11 ministries, tagging efforts have since expanded to cover all central government entities. Budget measures are tagged according to their contribution to 11 climate change activities. Measures are classified as either highly relevant (where more than 60% of programme budgets are allocated to one of the climate activities); relevant (where 20-60% of programme budgets are relevant); or neutral (where less than 20% of programme budgets are relevant). Sectoral ministries, in close co-ordination with the Ministry of Finance, tag proposed budgets through the Line Ministry Budget Information System, where it is reviewed and validated by the National Planning Committee. The results of tagged expenditures are presented as an annex to the budget document (Redbook) as well as in an annual citizens' climate budget.

Table 4. Nepal's green budget tagging "at a glance"

1.	Driven by national priorities	Climate change is a key policy priority of the government, particularly given its negative effects on the country's agricultural systems.
2.	Aligned to country-specific green goals	Climate expenditure tagging was introduced as part of the Climate Change Financing Framework, which mapped reforms in the public financial management system needed to improve climate budget accuracy and address sectoral nuances, improve accountability, and facilitate the evaluation of climate investments.
3.	Weighting system	Scaled – simplified approach to weighting. Expenditures are tagged when they are relevant to one of 11 climate activities. Measures are either highly relevant (where more than 60% of programme budgets are allocated to climate activities); relevant (where 20-60% of programme budgets are relevant); or neutral (where less than 20% of programme budgets are relevant).
4.	Work towards tagging both positive and negative budget measures	Captures only positive expenditures.
5.	Political commitment, leadership and clear roles/responsibilities	The National Planning Commission and the Ministry of Finance play key leadership roles.
6.	Guidance and process for review and validation	The National Planning Commission and the Ministry of Finance, as part of the budget process, provide guidelines for budget proposals, including requirements for line ministries to tag relevant expenditures within the budget system (Line Ministry Budget Information System).
7.	Tagging coincides with other tools that support green budgeting	
8.	Supported by modern budgetary governance framework	Nepal has a medium-term expenditure framework where tagged projects and programmes present a summary of budget estimations and expenditure projections. Nepal has programme-based budgeting allowing tagging to be conducted at a more granular activity level.
9.	Presented in green budget statement or citizens' budget	Climate change relevant expenditures are presented as an annex to the budget document (Redbook). A citizens' climate change budget is also published.
10.	Budget coincides with other public policy interventions	

Philippines

The Philippines introduced climate expenditure tagging in 2014, following a Climate Public Expenditure and Institutional Review in the previous year. The work was led by the Department of Budget and Management and the Philippines Climate Change Commission, with technical assistance from the World Bank with financial support from the Australia-World Bank Philippines Development Trust Fund. Climate expenditure tagging was introduced to help mobilise the financing needed to implement the country's planned Nationally Determined Contributions, in recognition of the need for progressive improvements in transparency in the planning, prioritisation, monitoring and reporting of climate action. Under the government's approach to climate tagging, expenditure that has climate change adaptation or mitigation explicitly as a main objective is tagged. For activities which partially address climate change, the proportion of the activity budget (relevant for climate change) is included in the tagging system. Expenditure is then further classified according to the country's National Climate Change Action Plan along sub-objectives and instrument categories.

The Department of Budget and Management along with the Climate Change Commission take lead roles in developing guidance and providing support to line ministries, which are responsible for tagging their expenditures into the budget proposal system. Validation is by the Climate Change Commission. Summary information is provided through briefs as part of the submission of the President's Budget to Congress.

Table 5. Philippine's green budget tagging "at a glance"

1.	Driven by national priorities	The frequency and intensity of typhoons, rising sea levels, variation in precipitation and rising temperatures have made the Philippines vulnerable to the impacts of climate change. This has propelled the government to enact the Climate Change Act (Republic Act 9729), which provided the policy framework to formulate strategy, mainstream climate risk into development plans and programmes, identify relevant instruments, and assess vulnerability across sectors. This helped set the basis for the National Climate Change Action Plan setting out national priorities from 2011 to 2028. Furthermore, in 2013, the Philippines, with the World Bank, conducted a Climate Public Expenditure and Institutional Review, where it recommended strengthening the planning, execution and financing framework for climate change; enhancing leadership and accountability through monitoring, evaluation and reviews of policies and activities; and building capacity in the government to manage change, setting the basis for budget tagging.
2.	Aligned to country-specific green goals	Expenditures are tagged in accordance to the National Climate Change Action Plan, which outlines several priorities and sub-priorities (food security, water sufficiency, ecosystem and environmental stability, human security, climate smart industries and services, sustainable energy, knowledge and capacity development, cross-cutting).
3.	Weighting system	Non-binary weighting. Programmes, activities and projects are counted in full if they primarily address climate change (mitigation or adaptation) as their main objective. For those which partially address climate change (mitigation or adaptation), the commensurate proportion of expenditure dedicated to climate change is counted.
4.	Work towards tagging both positive and negative budget measures	Only positive expenditures are tagged.
5.	Political commitment, leadership and clear roles/responsibilities	The Department of Budget and Management and the Climate Change Commission play key leading roles in taking forward climate expenditure tagging. In addition, the Department of the Interior and Local Government acts as the oversight agency for local climate expenditure tagging.
6.	Guidance and process for review and validation	Guidance is provided as part of the annual Budget Call by the Department of Budget and Management and through training on climate change expenditure tagging conducted by the Climate Change Commission. Validation checks on tagging are conducted by the Climate Change Commission (based on quality assurance review forms submitted by departments and agencies).
7.	Tagging coincides with other tools that support green budgeting	General provisions in the Annual Appropriations Act mandate agencies to ensure that programmes and projects included in the national budget give due consideration to the objectives of disaster risk reduction and climate change mitigation. In addition, the government has adopted a Program Convergence Budgeting approach, whereby government agencies work together to meet common objectives, instead of competing for budgets.
8.	Supported by modern budgetary governance framework	The Philippines introduced performance budgeting through the introduction of Public Expenditure Classification reforms from 2015 to 2018. These reforms helped to align the budget along appropriate programmes and strategies. Annual budgets contain performance information for all government programmes (in line with objectives, target outputs and indicators).
9.	Presented in green budget statement or citizens' budget	Climate budget reports are published by key climate change government agencies, with climate expenditure tables provided in the annual *Budget of Expenditures and Sources of Financing* publication submitted as part of the President's Budget to Congress. The Climate Change Commission also maintains a database on the country's climate change activities accessible through an online portal (https://niccdies.climate.gov.ph).
10.	Budget coincides with other public policy interventions	Green procurement, whereby public authorities seek to reduce the environmental impact associated with procured good, services and works throughout their life cycle, is currently being mainstreamed through the Philippine Green Public Procurement Roadmap.

References

AfDB et al. (2015), *2015 Joint Report on Multilateral Development Banks' Climate Finance*, Inter-American Development Bank, https://publications.iadb.org/en/2015-joint-report-multilateral-development-banks-climate-finance. [11]

Annukka, B. et al. (2019), *PATH2030 – An Evaluation of Finland's Sustainable Development Policy*. [54]

Climate Change Commission (2019), *Executive Brief: The Philippine National Climate Change Action Plan, Monitoring and Evaluation Report 2011-2016*, Climate Change Commission, Manila, https://climate.gov.ph/public/ckfinder/userfiles/files/Knowledge/The%20Philippine%20NCCAP%20M%26E%20Executive%20Brief_FINAL%20for%20Printing.pdf. [18]

Climate Change Commission (n.d.), *National Climate Change Action Plan 2011-2021*, Climate Change Commission, Manila. [19]

Coady, D. et al. (2019), "Global fossil fuel subsidies remain large: An update based on country-level estimates", *IMF Working Papers*, No. 19/89, International Monetary Fund, Washington, DC, https://www.imf.org/en/Publications/WP/Issues/2019/05/02/Global-Fossil-Fuel-Subsidies-Remain-Large-An-Update-Based-on-Country-Level-Estimates-46509. [58]

Cremins, A. and L. Kevany (2018), *An Introduction to the Implementation of Green Budgeting in Ireland*, Department of Public Expenditure and Reform, Dublin, https://igees.gov.ie/wp-content/uploads/2019/01/The-Implementation-of-Green-Budgeting-in-Ireland.pdf. [21]

Crepin, C. (2013), *Getting a Grip on Climate Change in the Philippines: Executive Report*, Public Expenditure Review, World Bank, Washington, DC, https://documents.worldbank.org/en/publication/documents-reports/documentdetail/473371468332663224/getting-a-grip-on-climate-change-in-the-philippines-executive-report. [36]

Danish Ministry of Climate, Energy and Utilities (2020), "Danish Climate Act passed by parliament with huge majority, enshrining 70% reduction target by 2030 in law", press release, Danish Ministry of Climate, Energy and Utilities, Copenhagen. [71]

de Bruin, K., E. Monaghan and A. Yakut (2019), "The impacts of removing fossil fuel subsidies and increasing carbon tax in Ireland", *ESRI Research Series* 98, http://aei.pitt.edu/102335/1/RS98.pdf. [55]

Department of Budget and Management (2020), *Asia Pacific Climate Budget Tagging Roundtable (23 June 2020)*. [39]

Downes, R. and S. Nicol (2019), *Designing and Implementing Gender Budgeting: A Path to Action*, OECD, Paris, https://www.oecd.org/gov/budgeting/designing-and-implementing-gender-budgeting-a-path-to-action.pdf. [63]

ESMAP (n.d.), "Energy Subsidy Reform Assessment Framework", webpage, Energy Sector Management Assistance Program, World Bank, Washington, DC, https://www.esmap.org/esraf. [59]

European Commission (2020), "EU taxonomy for sustainable activities", webpage, European Commission, https://ec.europa.eu/info/business-economy-euro/banking-and-finance/sustainable-finance/eu-taxonomy-sustainable-activities_en. [42]

European Commission (2018), "EU Taxonomy for Sustainable Activities", webpage, European Commission, https://ec.europa.eu/info/business-economy-euro/banking-and-finance/sustainable-finance/eu-taxonomy-sustainable-activities_en. [10]

European Commission et al. (2008), *System of National Accounts 2008*, United Nations, New York, https://unstats.un.org/unsd/nationalaccount/docs/SNA2008.pdf. [45]

Finnish Ministry of Finance (2019), *Draft Budget 2019*, Government of Finland, Helsinki. [53]

Frits, B. and A. Ruijs (2019), "Biodiversity in the Dutch practice of cost-benefit analysis", *CBP Background Document*, CPB Netherlands Bureau for Economic Policy Analysis, https://www.cpb.nl/sites/default/files/omnidownload/CPB-Background-Document-feb2019-Biodiversity-in-the-Dutch-practice-of-cost-benefit-analysis.pdf. [68]

Government of Canada (2019), *3rd Experts Meeting on Gender Budgeting*. [64]

Government of Colombia (2016), *Guía Metodológica para Clasificar y Medir el Financiamiento Asociado con Acciones de Mitigación y Adaptación al*, Government of Colombia, Bogota, https://mrv.dnp.gov.co/Publicaciones/Documents/GU%C3%8DA%20METODOL%C3%93GICA%20PARA%20CLASIFICAR%20Y%20MEDIR%20EL%20FINANCIAMIENTO%20ASOCIADO%20CON%20ACCIONES%20DE%20MITIGACI%C3%93N%20Y%20ADAPTACI%C3%93N.pdf. [27]

Government of France (2020), *Rapport sur l'impact environnemental du budget de l'État*, Government of France, Paris, https://www.budget.gouv.fr/files/uploads/extract/2021/PLF_2021/rapport_IEE.PDF. [60]

Government of France (2019), *Financement de la transition écologique: Les instruments économiques, fiscaux et budgétaires au service de l'environnement et du climat*, Government of France, Paris, https://www.performance-publique.budget.gouv.fr/sites/performance_publique/files/farandole/ressources/2020/pap/pdf/jaunes/Jaune2020_transition_ecologique.pdf (accessed on 7 January 2020). [51]

Government of Ghana (2018), *Climate Change Budget and Finance Tracking Manual*, Government of Ghana, Accra, https://www.gcfreadinessprogramme.org/sites/default/files/Revised%20Climate%20Finance%20Tracking%20Tool%202018.pdf. [40]

Haut Conseil pour le Climat (2019), *Evaluer les lois en cohérence avec les ambitions*, Haut Conseil pour le Climat, https://www.hautconseilclimat.fr/wp-content/uploads/2019/12/rapport-haut-conseil-pour-le-climat_evaluer-les-lois-en-cohrence-avec-les-ambitions-1.pdf. [31]

HM Treasury (2018), *The Green Book: Central Government Guidance on Appraisal and Evaluation*, HM Treasury, London, https://www.gov.uk/government/publications/the-green-book-appraisal-and-evaluation-in-central-governent. [6]

IADB (forthcoming), *Connections across Financial and Environmental Classifications Systems in the Context of Climate Change Public Budget Classification*, Inter-American Development Bank. [3]

ICMA (2018), *Green Bond Principles: Voluntary Process Guidelines for Issuing Green Bonds*, International Capital Market Association, Paris, https://www.icmagroup.org/assets/documents/Regulatory/Green-Bonds/Green-Bonds-Principles-June-2018-270520.pdf. [12]

IMF (2013), *Energy Subsidy Reform: Lessons and Implications*, International Monetary Fund, Washington, DC, https://www.imf.org/en/Publications/Policy-Papers/Issues/2016/12/31/Energy-Subsidy-Reform-Lessons-and-Implications-PP4741. [61]

Inderst, G., C. Kaminker and F. Stewart (2012), "Defining and measuring green investments: Implications for institutional investors' asset allocations", *OECD Working Papers on Finance, Insurance and Private Pensions*, No. 24, OECD Publishing, Paris, https://www.oecd.org/finance/WP_24_Defining_and_Measuring_Green_Investments.pdf. [9]

Italian Ministry of Environment, Land and Sea (2017), *Catalogo Dei Sussidi Ambientalmente Favorevoli e Dei Sussidi Ambientalmente Dannosi 2016 (Catalogue of Environmentally Friendly and Environmentally Harmful Subsidies 2016)*, Italian Ministry of Environment, Land and Sea, Rome, https://www.minambiente.it/pagina/economia-ambientale (accessed on 24 January 2020). [15]

Ministry of Finance of Bangladesh (2020), *Climate FInancing for Sustainable Development*, Government of Bangladesh, https://mof.gov.bd/site/page/c8152900-0839-44b5-b271-4414cbc2b9ab/Climate. [52]

Ministry of the Ecological Transition (2020), "Green budgeting in France", presentation at the OECD Paris Collaborative Meeting on 17 March 2020, Ministry of the Ecological Transition, Paris. [20]

Nepalese Ministry of Agriculture (2020), "Experience and role of climate budget tagging in mainstreaming climate change in public financial management", presentation at Asia-Pacific Roundtable. [34]

New Zealand Government (2019), "Climate change lens on major government decisions", press release, New Zealand Government, Wellington, https://www.beehive.govt.nz/release/climate-change-lens-major-government-decisions. [72]

OECD (2020), *OECD Analysis of Budgetary Support and Tax Expenditures*, OECD, Paris, http://www.oecd.org/fossil-fuels/data. [56]

OECD (2020), *OECD Green Budgeting Framework*, OECD, Paris, http://www.oecd.org/environment/green-budgeting/OECD-Green-Budgeting-Framework-Highlights.pdf. [1]

OECD (2020), *OECD Inventory of Support Measures for Fossil Fuels*, OECD, Paris, https://stats.oecd.org/Index.aspx?DataSetCode=FFS_AUS. [57]

OECD (2020), *Tracking Economic Instruments and Finance for Biodiversity*, OECD, Paris, http://www.oecd.org/environment/resources/tracking-economic-instruments-and-finance-for-biodiversity-2020.pdf. [25]

OECD (2019), *Biodiversity: Finance and the Economic and Business Case for Action*, report prepared for the G7 Finance Ministers' Meeting, 5-6 May 2019, OECD, Paris, https://www.oecd.org/environment/resources/biodiversity/G7-report-Biodiversity-Finance-and-the-Economic-and-Business-Case-for-Action.pdf. [69]

OECD (2019), *Budgeting and Public Expenditures in OECD Countries 2019*, OECD Publishing, Paris, https://dx.doi.org/10.1787/9789264307957-en. [50]

OECD (2019), *Budgeting and Public Expenditures in OECD Countries 2019*, OECD Publishing, Paris, https://dx.doi.org/10.1787/9789264307957-en. [66]

OECD (2019), *OECD Good Practices for Performance Budgeting*, OECD Publishing, Paris, https://doi.org/10.1787/c90b0305-en. [49]

OECD (2019), *OECD Scan: Equality Budgeting in Ireland*, OECD, Paris, https://www.oecd.org/gov/budgeting/equality-budgeting-in-ireland.pdf. [38]

OECD (2019), *Reforming Public Procurement: Progress in Implementing the 2015 OECD Recommendation*, OECD Public Governance Reviews, OECD Publishing, Paris, https://dx.doi.org/10.1787/1de41738-en. [16]

OECD (2018), *Cost-Benefit Analysis and the Environment: Further Developments and Policy Use*, OECD Publishing, Paris, https://dx.doi.org/10.1787/9789264085169-en. [48]

OECD (2018), *Gender Equality in Canada: Mainstreaming, Governance and Budgeting*, OECD Publishing, Paris, https://dx.doi.org/10.1787/9789264301108-en. [65]

OECD (2018), *Mainstreaming Biodiversity for Sustainable Development*, OECD Publishing, Paris, https://dx.doi.org/10.1787/9789264303201-en. [24]

OECD (2017), *Policy Instruments for the Environment*, OECD, Paris, https://www.oecd.org/environment/tools-evaluation/PINE_database_brochure.pdf. [44]

OECD (2016), *OECD-DAC Rio Markers for Climate Handbook*, OECD, Paris, https://www.oecd.org/dac/environment-development/Revised%20climate%20marker%20handbook_FINAL.pdf. [13]

OECD (2015), *Going Green: Best Pratices for Sustainable Procurement*, OECD, Paris, https://www.oecd.org/gov/public-procurement/Going_Green_Best_Practices_for_Sustainable_Procurement.pdf. [70]

OECD (2011), *OECD DAC Rio Markers for Climate Handbook*, OECD, Paris, https://www.oecd.org/dac/environment-development/Revised%20climate%20marker%20handbook_FINAL.pdf. [28]

OECD (2004), *OECD Glossary of Statistical Terms*, OECD, Paris, https://stats.oecd.org/glossary/glossary.pdf. [46]

OECD (n.d.), *Climate-related Development Finance Data*, OECD, Paris, http://www.oecd.org/dac/financing-sustainable-development/development-finance-topics/Climate-related-development-finance-in-2018.pdf. [41]

OECD (forthcoming), *The Green Budget Statement*, OECD, Paris, forthcoming. [17]

Pakistani Controller General of Accounts (2020), "Experience and role of climate budget tagging in mainstreaming climate change in public financial management", presentation at Asia-Pacific Roundtable. [33]

Petri, H. (2017), "Short guide to the use of Rio markers", webpage, European Union, https://europa.eu/capacity4dev/public-environment-climate/wiki/short-guide-use-rio-markers?cookies=disabled. [29]

Pradhan, S. (1996), "Evaluating spending: A framework for public expenditure reviews", *World Bank Discussion Papers*, WDP 323, World Bank Group, Washington, DC, http://documents.worldbank.org/curated/en/509221468740209997/Evaluating-public-spending-a-framework-for-public-expenditure-reviews. [5]

Resch, E. et al. (2017), "Mainstreaming, accessing and institutionalising finance for climate change adaptation", *Action on Climate Today Learning Paper*, https://reliefweb.int/report/world/mainstreaming-accessing-and-institutionalising-finance-climate-change-adaptation. [30]

Schaffitzel, F. et al. (2019), *Can Government Transfers Make Energy Subsidy Reform Socially Acceptable? A Case Study on Ecuador*, Inter-American Development Bank, http://dx.doi.org/10.18235/0001740. [62]

Stotsky, J. (2016), "Gender budgeting: Fiscal context and current outcomes", *IMF Working Papers*, No. 16/149, International Monetary Fund, Washington, DC, https://www.imf.org/en/Publications/WP/Issues/2016/12/31/Gender-Budgeting-Fiscal-Context-and-Current-Outcomes-44132. [67]

Swedish Ministry of the Environment and Energy (2018), *The Swedish Cliamte Policy Framework*, Government Offices of Sweden, Stcokholm, https://www.government.se/495f60/contentassets/883ae8e123bc4e42aa8d59296ebe0478/the-swedish-climate-policy-framework.pdf. [32]

Umweltbundesamt (2016), *Umweltschädliche Subventionen in Deutschland*, Umweltbundesamt, https://www.umweltbundesamt.de/publikationen (accessed on 24 January 2020). [14]

UN et al. (2014), *System of Environmental Accounting 2012 - Central Framework*, United Nations, New York, https://seea.un.org/sites/seea.un.org/files/seea_cf_final_en.pdf. [47]

UNDP (2019), "Knowing what you spend: A guidance note for governments to track climate finance in their budgets", *Climate Change Financing Framework Technical Note Series*, United Nations Development Programme, https://www.undp.org/content/undp/en/home/librarypage/climate-and-disaster-resilience-/knowing-what-you-spend.html. [8]

UNDP (2015), *Climate Budget Tagging: The Case Studies of Bangladesh, Indonesia, Nepal and the Philippines*, United Nations Development Programme, https://www.climatefinance-developmenteffectiveness.org/sites/default/files/event/CFSDforum2015/climate/Climate%20Budget%20Tagging%20_July%202015_DRAFT.pdf. [37]

UNFCCC (2020), "Nationally Determined Contributions (NDCs)", webpage, United Nations Framework Convention on Climate Change, https://unfccc.int/process-and-meetings/the-paris-agreement/the-paris-agreement/nationally-determined-contributions-ndcs. [4]

United Nations (2020), "Disaster risk management", webpage, United Nations Office for Outer Space Affairs, http://www.un-spider.org/risks-and-disasters/disaster-risk-management. [26]

US EPA (2017), "Air quality management process cycle", webpage, United States Environmental Protection Agency, Washington, DC, https://www.epa.gov/air-quality-management-process/air-quality-management-process-cycle. [22]

Weikmans, R. et al. (2017), "Assessing the credibility of how climate adaptation aid projects are categorised", *Development in Practice*, Vol. 27/4, pp. 458-471, http://dx.doi.org/10.1080/09614524.2017.1307325. [35]

World Bank (2014), *Climate Change Public Expenditure and Institutional Review Sourcebook*, World Bank Group, Washington, DC, https://www.greenfinanceplatform.org/sites/default/files/downloads/resource/World_Bank_CC_PEIR_Sourcebook_0.pdf. [7]

World Bank (2011), *Tracking Activities with Climate Co-benefits – MDB Experience*, World Bank, Washington, DC, http://www.oecd.org/env/cc/48251339.pdf. [43]

World Bank (forthcoming), *Climate Change Expenditure Tagging: An Overview of Current Practices*, World Bank, Washington, DC, forthcoming. [2]

World Bank (n.d.), "Water resources management", webpage, World Bank, Washington, DC, https://www.worldbank.org/en/topic/waterresourcesmanagement#2. [23]

Notes

[1] Green bonds are bonds that signify a commitment to exclusively use the funds to finance or refinance "green" projects, assets or business activities.

[2] The Central Budget Authority is a public entity, or several co-ordinated entities, located at the central/national/federal level of government, which is responsible for budget formulation and oversight. In many countries, the CBA is often found within or coincides with the Ministry of Finance/Economy. In many instances, Ministries of Planning also share a leading role with the CBA.

[3] Codes often reflect a typology of budget items in relation to their green objective (e.g. climate change mitigation), sub-objective, identification of instrument (e.g. research or service delivery) and its corresponding activity. In the Philippines, for example, a Climate Change Expenditure Typology reflects six numbers and letters each reflecting an area of categorisation (e.g. AI24-01, where A identifies the budget as one addressing climate change adaptation, I representing a priority within the country's action plan, 2 representing a sub-priority, 4 representing the type of instrument used and 01 representing the activity).

[4] See: http://oe.cd/pine.

[5] An exception is the EU taxonomy which was made alongside the Statistical Classification of Economic Activities in the European Community (NACE).

[6] PINE is an OECD database gathering key quantitative and qualitative information on policy instruments relevant to environmental and natural resource management across 80 countries.

[7] Note, mitigation spend may also have negative externalities.